GW01417525

Courts Unmasked

Courts Unmasked

Civil Legal System Reform
and COVID-19

Alyx Mark

University Press of Kansas

This book will be made open access within three years of publication thanks to Path to Open, a program developed in partnership between JSTOR, the American Council of Learned Societies (ACLS), University of Michigan Press, and the University of North Carolina Press to bring about equitable access and impact for the entire scholarly community, including authors, researchers, libraries, and university presses around the world. Learn more at https://about.jstor.org/path-to-open/.

Published by the University Press of Kansas (Lawrence, Kansas 66045), which was organized by the Kansas Board of Regents and is operated and funded by Emporia State University, Fort Hays State University, Kansas State University, Pittsburg State University, the University of Kansas, and Wichita State University.

Library of Congress Cataloging-in-Publication Data

Names: Mark, Alyx, author.
Title: Courts unmasked : civil legal system reform and COVID-19 / Alyx Mark.
Description: Lawrence : University Press of Kansas, 2024. | Includes
    bibliographical references and index.
Identifiers: LCCN 2024023146 (print) | LCCN 2024023147 (ebook) |
    ISBN 9780700638253 (cloth) |
    ISBN 9780700638260 (paperback) |
    ISBN 9780700638277 (ebook)
Subjects: LCSH: Courts–United States–States. | Courts of last resort–United
    States–States. | Law reform–United States–States. | Administrative courts–
    United States–States. | COVID-19 (Disease)–Law and legislation–United
    States–States. | COVID-19 Pandemic, 2020–United States.
Classification: LCC KF8736 .M37 2024 (print) | LCC KF8736 (ebook) |
    DDC 347.73/309052–dc23/eng/20240528
LC record available at https://lccn.loc.gov/2024023146.
LC ebook record available at https://lccn.loc.gov/2024023147.

British Library Cataloguing-in-Publication Data is available.

To Z.Z. and M.M.
for your support in all things, always

Contents

Preface

A tenant discovers a bloom of mold in the bathroom of their rental apartment. A collector is demanding the payment of an unfamiliar debt. A vehicle is totaled in a head-on collision and one driver is uninsured. A single parent is seeking child support that is past due. A minimum-wage worker is fired after an on-the-job injury.

Civil justice problems like these bring tens of millions of people through the doors of state courts in the United States each year. The vast majority of these people go it alone, without the assistance of legal representation. In these courthouses, parties will file claims and answers to dispute them, pay fines and fees, seek legal information, and attend hearings.

All of that matters. It matters to the people trying to navigate the system, it matters to the court staff trying to do their jobs, and it matters to scholars, researchers, and advocates who care about our legal system and democratic institutions. Court rules and processes play a critical role in a person's ability to successfully navigate the civil legal system and resolve their problems. The rules can determine whether tenants and landlords are routed to the courtroom or to a mediation program that could prevent an eviction. The rules dictate whether a worker must take a day off work and arrange childcare for an in-person hearing or if they can appear in court remotely. The rules even determine whether an underbanked person will need to borrow money for a cashier's check in order to pay a court fee or if they can easily apply for a fee waiver. The choice between the adoption of one policy or another can have a significant impact on the resolution of a person's immediate legal problem. It may also have lasting effects on the health, well-being, and security of both the individual and their families and communities.

It is my hope that this book helps us to "unmask" courts' administrative choices by exploring the reasons behind their operational decisions and the factors that influence how they approach the resolution of civil legal problems. I have been a student of state civil courts for more than a decade, principally studying how judges, lawyers, lay advocates, and the self-represented navigate the intricacies of the institutional frameworks they find themselves working within. This project represents an interest—and an opportunity—to study what goes in to shaping those contexts from both the perspective of those at the top of the hierarchy and those who work tirelessly in our trial courts to apply rules and procedure to the overwhelming circumstances they find themselves within.

Acknowledgments

First, to David Congdon, my editor at the University Press of Kansas: It is unlikely that I would be typing up these acknowledgments if it wasn't for your e-mail back in 2021 asking me if I was thinking about writing a book about this work. Thank you for helping me see this project's potential. To Michael Nelson and Amanda Driscoll, thank you for organizing the "COVID-19 Pandemic and Judicial Politics" panel at the 2021 meeting of the Midwest Political Science Association, which was very much the springboard for this entire enterprise. To Delia Lloyd, you pushed me out of my comfort zone, shook me out of my writing blocks, and cheered me on. Thank you for helping me realize that this was something I could do.

It is difficult for me to imagine how this project would have come to fruition without the support of a number of organizations, academic institutions, colleagues, friends, and family members. Thanks to the National Science Foundation, the Pew Charitable Trusts, the American Association of University Women, and Wesleyan University for financial support and the invaluable gift of time.

To Ricardo Lillo and the Faculty of Law at Universidad Adolfo Ibáñez; Paulo Alves da Silva and the University of São Paulo–Law School of Ribeirão Preto; Virginia Hettinger and the Political Science Department at the University of Connecticut; México Evalúa; Adam Zimmerman and Loyola Law School; Sharyn Roach Anleu, João Paulo Dias, Paula Casaleiro, and Leire Kortabarria at the Oñati International Institute for the Sociology of Law; Emily Taylor Poppe at the UC Irvine School of Law; and Nigel Balmer of the Victoria Law Foundation, New York University's Center on Civil Justice, and AAUW's Lower Connecticut Valley and Shoreline chapters—thank you for inviting me to share drafts with a range of thoughtful audiences across the globe. I am also grateful to the anonymous reviewers of the book manuscript and at the Oñati Sociolegal Series, Lisa Holmes, Lauren C. Bell, members of the Law and Courts Women's Writing Group, The Hon. Anthony Mohr (Ret.), the editorial board of the University Press of Kansas, the American Bar Association's *Judges Journal*, and conference participants at meetings of the Midwest and Southern Political Science Associations for their comments and questions. Your helpful feedback has played a key role in shaping this project.

I also thank the Oñati International Institute for the Sociology of Law for permission to reprint material in this book that first appeared as "Perceptions of Administrative Policymaking Authority: Evidence from Interviews in Three State Court Systems," in the *Oñati Sociolegal Series* S13: S171–S198. This material principally appears in chapter 3. In addition, I thank the American Bar Association for permission to reprint material in this book that first appeared as "Pandemic Policymaking in State Supreme Courts: Implications for the Administration of Justice" in the Summer 2024 issue of the *Judges Journal*. This material primarily appears in chapter 1.

A number of experts graciously lent me their ears, eyes, and brains in the moments I felt like everything was on fire—despite their own demanding workloads. Thank you to Valerie Nazzaro and Pavel Oleinikov at Wesleyan University's Quantitative Analysis Center for your deep wells of methodological knowledge and the countless hours of moral support as we wrestled with the data throughout the writing process, to Qudsiya Naqui and Erika Rickard at Pew for your attentive engagement with the substance of the project, and to Justin Weinstein-Tull for providing an archived version of the NCSC's 2016 State Court Organization survey data, Gaines Elmore for your data visualization wizardry, and the ABA's COVID-19 Task Force for its assistance with connecting me to the judges and court staff of countless jurisdictions across the United States who provided insights and reflections that were critical to the success of the project.

This project would also not have been possible without an amazing team of research assistants, at both Wesleyan University and Columbia Law School. Thanks to Mo'ath Almahasneh, Armando Alvarez, Sarah Bernstein, Michelle Bigony (CLS), Tiger Bjornlund, Alex Brun, Izzy Bush, Liam Caplan, Julia Crainic, Juliet Dale, Max Duerr, Maggie Eames, Betsy Froiland, Zoe Genden, Arnaud Gerlus, Sophia Goh (CLS), Hannah Goncher, Ned Herrington, Lucy Howland, Annie McGovern, Amanda McHugh, Charlie McPhee, Grace Melville, Macy Miller, Elizabeth Myers, Ji Yoon Park, Sara Parmet, Mason Polaner, Gabby Roberts, Oliver Saffery, Spencer Saunders, Connor Shaw, Gabe Siegel, Andrew Simard, Emily Smith, Preksha Sreewastav, Sally Tepper, Sophia Trombold, Mason Walther (CLS), Justin Weinstein, and Kiarah Young for your dedication to advancing the project.

Turning to my friends and family—to my Wesleyan crew, people who now know quite a lot about the administration of state civil courts, possibly more than they'd like: Sonali Chakravarti, Logan Dancey, Lindsay Dolan, Erika Franklin Fowler, Nina Hagel, Alexis May, Justin Peck, Hari Ramesh, and Lauren Silber; lifelong friends from graduate school who are still willing to lend their expertise and help me see the forest for the trees: Jessie Anderson, Dani Gilbert, Jake Haselswerdt, and Dillon Stone Tatum; friends who might as well be family, for checking in and indulging my ramblings: Carol and Greg Brown, Erin Brown, Leslie and Aaron Chenoweth, Jacqueline Kull, Brian McKenzie, and Kenny Nisbet and Set Oya; my longtime collaborators and confidantes Colleen Shanahan, Anna Carpenter, and Jessica Steinberg; and to my family, Stephanie, Randy, Tyler and Jack Cann, Michael Mark and Denise Foutch, and Teryl and David Zarnow—your reserves of patience, love, and kindness were seemingly inexhaustible. Thank you all for generously sharing with me and holding space for me when I needed it. I hope to return the favor someday.

And finally, to Zach. You know what you did. Because it was everything.

Introduction

The COVID-19 pandemic changed the work practices of nearly every industry around the globe, forcing institutions to quickly adapt to the evolving public health emergency. State court systems in the United States were no exception. Courts developed strategies to reconfigure their approaches to processing cases, frequently utilizing technology to serve court users remotely. Notwithstanding the preexisting integration of technology in many courts, the pandemic acted as an accelerant, fostering the rapid, widespread adoption of tools long championed by civil justice reformers. The changes made to court operations and case processing rules in response to the pandemic have also brought to light significant differences in how state court systems design and implement policies that affect the administration of justice. These differences challenge our existing understanding of how administrative policymaking occurs in courts.

The developments in state courts during the pandemic mark a monumental escalation of a broader dialogue about procedural reform in courts. The shift to remote appearances in hearings, for example, was a proposal that had long been supported by advocates and court leaders (e.g., Legal Services Corporation 2013)—well before lockdowns and social distancing measures were enforced. It was also a proposal that had been road-tested—many state court systems had some level of experience incorporating audiovisual technologies in their hearings, most commonly employing them in the context of pre-trial hearings for those in custody and for other criminal matters (Seidman-Diamond et al. 2010; Spillane 2021, 541–42; Turner 2021).[1] Some courts had also used these technologies to enable witness testimony from individuals located in other states or countries, offer remote language interpretation, and conduct certain pre-trial hearings in civil cases (Lederer 2021,

316–319) as well as to enable more cost-effective participation in hearings by those living in remote rural areas (see Cabral et al. 2012). A smaller number of courts were experimenting with online dispute resolution platforms for specific case types, such as small claims, traffic, and debt cases.[2] What distinguishes the pandemic moment from these instances is the nearly universal sense of urgency it instilled to design and implement such reforms across all state court systems in the United States.

Consequently, irrespective of their experience incorporating technology in their operations before the pandemic, responding to COVID-19 required court systems and the individual courts within them to develop plans that would allow them to broadly serve their communities from a distance. In some states, supreme courts leveraged their positions as the chief administrators of their branches and took a top-down approach to pandemic response, giving themselves considerable control over their systems' transitions to the remote environment. In others, supreme courts took an approach that reflected how administrative authority was distributed across their systems, granting lower courts the flexibility to adopt policies suitable for their local circumstances. For example, in the case of remote hearings practices, early orders from high courts in Kentucky and Massachusetts took a top-down approach, instructing lower courts to permit remote participation by parties and attorneys in the hearing types they prioritized early in the pandemic,[3] while high courts in Florida and Missouri offered more flexibility to lower courts in their early pandemic orders, permitting presiding or chief judges of lower courts to decide if remote hearings were appropriate across similar categories of cases.

Orders that served to constrain or empower lower court actors led to higher and lower levels of uniformity in the policy decisions these courts made regarding the use of remote hearing modalities. Lower courts in Kentucky and Massachusetts tended to adopt language that signaled that they were constrained by the orders of their respective supreme courts. For example, administrative orders distributed early in the pandemic by Kentucky's trial courts instructed judges to conduct all proceedings remotely, specifically attributing this policy choice to provisions that were made explicit in their Supreme Court's orders.[4] Similarly, in Massachusetts, lower courts issued orders mandating that emergency matters be conducted solely through remote technologies.[5] To note, in both states, supreme court orders offered lower court judges in managerial positions limited discretion to make choices about the use of remote technologies in their jurisdictions.[6] However, the orders promulgated in these lower courts did not significantly differ from those circulated by their respective supreme courts. These lower court orders emphasized the use of remote methods as the primary means of conducting essential hearings, with in-person proceedings being the exception rather than the rule.[7]

In contrast, lower courts in Florida and Missouri interpreted the discretion granted to them in their supreme courts' orders as empowering them to develop the administrative policies they deemed most appropriate. Early orders distributed by trial courts in Florida interpreted their high court's wishes liberally, including language that offered judges in their jurisdictions considerable discretion to make decisions about the appropriateness of remote hearings at the individual level—permitting judges to determine "when," "if," or "wherever" such hearings would be possible or practicable.[8] Lower court orders in Florida also seemed to turn their Supreme Court's guidance on its head, permitting remote hearings in essential matters *only* upon the approval of a chief judge.[9]

Missouri's lower courts also varied in how they interpreted their Supreme Court's permission to determine when to offer remote options. Some courts "strongly encouraged and recommended" remote proceedings in their early orders.[10] Others were more explicit regarding the use of remote methods, promulgating orders requiring that hearings be conducted online unless a judge could offer evidence that a hearing could not be fairly conducted in a remote environment or stating that there would be no in-person proceedings for essential hearings (with some exceptions).[11] But others were looser in their approach, offering each judge the discretion to "hear . . . matters via telephone or videoconferencing"[12] or to otherwise "take appropriate action"[13] aligned with the lower court's broad recommendations pertaining to court operations, with no specific mention of how judges should proceed with their hearings.

The COVID-19 pandemic forced a swift transformation of court operations in order to minimize disruptions to the services provided to their users and revealed considerable variation in how state court systems approach administrative decision-making in the process. In these examples, the high courts of Kentucky and Massachusetts employed a more hierarchical approach to managing the administration of their courts, and lower court orders reflected their supreme courts' preferences over the use of remote technologies for various hearing types. In contrast, Florida and Missouri's high courts gave greater flexibility to their lower courts, resulting in more diverse interpretations of their orders. These observations lead to questions regarding the factors that shape the design and implementation of the policies that govern court operations.

Whether procedures are established by a central authority or determined locally by individual courts, the locus of such decision-making in a state court system can influence the experiences of individuals both within and across jurisdictions. Even temporary changes to the rules surrounding the participation of parties and other participants in hearings, as well as rules regarding the initiation of cases, the filing and verification of court documents, the notification of defendants in lawsuits, and the scheduling of hearings, can significantly impact the ability of people to effectively navigate the legal system to address their legal problems (e.g., Rickard 2017).

The circumstances of the COVID-19 pandemic undeniably propelled state court systems to implement swift and substantial modifications to various administrative processes. Many of these changes were reflective of civil justice reform advocates' calls for procedural change. Courts themselves also recognized that such modifications may result in a more responsive and efficient legal system. Despite with the substantial impact of these administrative choices on everyday court users and court operations, both in and out of the pandemic context, our understanding of how these decisions are made and updated within and across state court systems in the United States remains limited. Therefore, it becomes critical to examine who makes these decisions and how they are implemented.

Understanding Patterns of Procedural Change in State Courts during the Pandemic Era

Prior to the pandemic, it was challenging to conduct empirical research on patterns of administrative decision-making in state court systems. Prospective modifications to generally applicable court procedures, such as to the rules regarding remote participation in hearings, may have been piloted and evaluated on a smaller scale by individual states or clusters of jurisdictions within states before being offered to their state judiciaries' rulemaking bodies for consideration as meaningful improvements. But before March 2020, these projects—especially those leveraging technology—were not undertaken in ways that allowed for meaningful comparisons across states. As a result, our ability to empirically assess how changes to court processes came about before the pandemic was limited to describing specific examples of change (e.g., Farley, Jensen, and Rempel 2014; Brinkman 2007; Krimmel 1993; Lee et al. 2013; Berkson and Hays 1976). A unique opportunity arises with the surge of updates to court processes induced by the pandemic, allowing for the capture, description, and explanation of patterns of procedural change in American state courts, offering the potential to better understand the participation of individuals in these processes and how their participation is influenced by their institutional contexts.

The study of administrative policy choices in courts is challenging not only because of the complexities of empirical research, but also because of a split in the focus of scholars. There is a lack of consensus on how to theorize about the determinants of the administrative choices made by those working in courts. Historically, one body of work has examined the causes and consequences of decisions that are made in cases, or adjudicatory decisions. Another has focused on the study of the choices that route those cases through the legal system, or a judiciary's administrative choices. The former camp speaks in the language of hierarchies, emphasizing the top-down power of supreme courts in defining the boundaries of acceptable legal judgments for all other courts under their jurisdiction. The latter group tends to emphasize that many of the administrative decisions courts make are highly localized. They stress the role of the individual jurisdiction or judge in the ways the rules of case processing are implemented.

However, this is not to say that hierarchical logics are irrelevant to the administrative policymaking process. Formal systems of designing and adopting procedural rules often vest significant power in state supreme courts (see generally Vining and Wilhelm 2023). Indeed, many supreme courts relied upon "chief administrator" justifications in managing their systems' responses to the pandemic (Mark 2024). But high courts may vary in the types of policies they choose to adopt, conveying their preferences through the use of administrative policy tools that constrain or empower lower courts to varying degrees. As evidenced in the above examples, jurisdiction-specific indicators may also play a role in the implementation decisions made by lower courts. Under normal circumstances, there have been limited opportunities to observe how these hierarchical and local factors interact in court systems' administrative decision-making processes. This book proposes that analyzing administrative decision-making during the COVID-19 pandemic using these two theoretical frameworks can provide valuable insights into the diverse approaches to procedural governance employed in court systems. Through this analysis, we can extract insights from the pandemic experience and apply those lessons to future policymaking decisions, enhancing our understanding of procedural governance in court systems.

To examine how the power to make the administrative policies that govern case processing and court operations is distributed in state courts, I employ a multi-method research design. I explore patterns of procedural policy change through analyses of courts' administrative orders and similar policy documents alongside in-depth interviews and a review of secondary literature. My data include a comprehensive collection of state court orders and guidance from the first year of the pandemic era (March 2020 to April 2021); interviews with nearly sixty court actors, including clerks, judges, and court administrators across three illustrative case study states; and a collection of permanent procedural changes made and under consideration in fifteen states representative of the range of approaches taken to pandemic-era procedural policymaking in state court systems.

Through these empirical exercises, I find that patterns of the design and implementation of policies that govern court operations are reflective of two factors: one that is informed by the way administrative power is formally structured in state courts and one that is informed by court actors' perceptions of their local environments. Structurally speaking, in systems where formal administrative power is performed in a highly centralized way, we observe fewer opportunities for the development of locally applicable processes, as policies tend to be designed by actors at the top of court hierarchies and are then implemented by those working in the courts below. Conversely, in systems where power is more horizontally distributed across actors in a variety of roles across court levels, we observe more opportunities for the development of local approaches to case processing as more actors are formally empowered to make policy.

In terms of the perceptual factor, I examine the behavior of actors working in lower courts and find that they do not always behave in ways that conform to the administrative power structures in their states. Their decisions to follow or deviate from high courts' administrative policies are influenced by their perceptions of the need to tailor their operational policies to their local environments, even in the absence of formal authority to do so. We may observe these decisions take shape in formalized policies, like local administrative orders, when lower courts are permitted to promulgate them. However, even in cases where lower courts lack the formal authority to deviate from the high court's administrative policies, they may make informal choices at the individual actor level to accommodate their local contexts. Detecting these unofficial behaviors is challenging without using an interview-based approach to data collection.

This book seeks to motivate the development of a theoretical approach to understanding how court systems establish and enforce policies regarding their operations by integrating and empirically assessing hierarchical and more localized accounts of court actors' decision-making. Emphasizing the significance of studying courts' administrative policy through these two lenses, the book relies on novel data and a diverse set of analysis techniques to offer evidence of these dynamic processes. The book aims to enrich an ongoing conversation among scholars and practitioners on civil justice reform and serve as a valuable resource for understanding how court system characteristics shape the development of administrative policy innovations and litigants' experiences working within various procedural regimes.

The subsequent sections of this introduction are structured in the following way: First, I distinguish between criminal and civil courts and explain why this project primarily focuses on the civil legal system, I illustrate the types of cases that fall under this category, and I provide insights into the workload of state civil courts. Next, I introduce my argument, which challenges the conventional approach of separating explanations of adjudicative and administrative processes in courts and advocates for their complementary nature. I present a novel framework for analyzing procedural policymaking authority that encompasses both hierarchical and more horizontal power structures observed in state courts. Then, I offer a brief overview of the book's methodology and preview some of its major findings. Following a discussion of the book's contribution to both scholarly and practical domains, I conclude with a road map of the upcoming chapters.

Why This Book Focuses on the Rules and Processes Governing State Civil Courts

This section briefly describes the differences between the criminal and civil legal systems and serves to justify the book's focus on understanding the processes and operational choices that facilitate the resolution of civil legal problems in state courts.

Although the policy changes described in this book may have affected the processing of both civil and criminal cases, the book will not focus on policy choices that are exclusively related to the operations of the criminal legal system. This choice is based on the unique circumstances under which individuals interact with the criminal or civil legal system, as well as the distinct rights afforded to them in each setting. The section also discusses the challenges faced by court users who proceed without representation in civil cases and how these challenges differ from the criminal court user. Finally, the section explores the impact of the COVID-19 pandemic on the user-friendliness of state civil courts and the potential implications of procedural change for lay litigants.

An important distinction between the criminal and civil legal systems stems from a contrast in the purpose of the two (Klein 1999; Mann 1991). The civil legal system was set up by the state as a platform for private parties to resolve their civil legal disputes and otherwise make claims to their private rights backed by the force of law. In contrast, in the criminal system parties are typically defending themselves against an allegation of an action committed *against* the state. The different purposes of the two shape the nature of the dealings people have with a particular system. Given its design, contact with the criminal justice system is wholly compulsory: if a person has allegedly committed an action prohibited by the state (e.g., burglary, embezzlement, sexual assault) and the state initiates criminal charges, the accused is forced to participate. In contrast, if a person is seeking to obtain a divorce, a civil order of protection from an abusive partner, enforce the terms of a contract, receive compensation for an injury resulting from negligent behavior, or otherwise seek a legal resolution of a dispute with another private party, they must opt *in* to using the civil legal system to obtain a private good. But there is also a compulsory element present in the civil legal system—if one elects to use it, one must also play by its rules.

In both the criminal and civil legal systems, these rules have been (in large part) designed by those with law degrees to be used by fellow members of the legal profession (Rickard 2017;

Shanahan, Carpenter, and Mark 2016; Carpenter et al. 2018, 2022b). These rules are generally not written in ways that are accessible to the average court user. This leads to another important difference between the two systems—in the criminal legal system, defendants are constitutionally entitled to an attorney. In other words, there is a guarantee of help with the interpretation of the law for those who interact with this system. And while there are plenty of reasonable critiques of public defense in the United States (e.g., Richardson and Goff 2013; but see Cole 1999; Butler 2013), in the civil legal system there is no such guarantee.

Each year, around fifteen million civil cases are initiated in state courts.[14] In many jurisdictions, the vast majority of people engage in these disputes proceed without representation—in some jurisdictions, civil dockets are overwhelmed by unrepresented parties on both sides of disputes (Shanahan et al. 2022a).[15] In spite of the high likelihood of a court user navigating a system designed for attorneys without one, law and process have largely not adapted to the users that civil courts serve (see generally Shanahan et al. 2022a; Buenger 2020; Spaulding 2020; Rickard 2017). As a consequence, people who access courts without lawyers often fail to successfully navigate procedure and court rules. Parties without lawyers have a higher probability of defaulting on the procedural responsibilities they must carry out in order to have their cases heard and resolved by a court.[16] And, these failures and errors can occur at every stage of the civil legal process—from failures to file complaints and answers "completely and correctly" to finalizing and implementing the judgments of the court (see also Hannaford-Agor 2003).[17] It follows that if a litigant is unaware of the rules of the game, it becomes difficult to play by them (e.g., Shanahan, Carpenter, and Mark 2016; see also Galanter 1974).

Many of the temporary changes to process that courts made during the pandemic have the potential to improve the user-friendliness of these institutions in the post-pandemic period (Zarnow and Hirsch 2021; Cabral et al. 2012). Such changes may serve to make it more convenient for people to use courts via remote services[18] and easier for those to participate who were previously unable to fully engage in an in-person setting (Shanahan et al. 2020; see also Steinberg 2015; Barton 2010).[19] The pandemic has been a major catalyst for innovation in the legal system. Numerous innovations, which might not have been adopted at such a large scale or with such speed under normal circumstances (Pew Charitable Trusts 2021), have emerged due to the actions of supreme courts and, in some cases, in spite of them.

For those navigating the legal system with the help of a lawyer, procedural change may not create significant changes to the process of solving a legal problem, as the baseline knowledge advocates have may make it easier for them to both anticipate and accommodate change (Galanter 1974; Shanahan, Carpenter, and Mark 2016). For the lay litigant, there is no such foundation. Further, if a person has a civil justice problem that requires resolution at a time when the barriers to participation are in flux, like during the COVID-19 pandemic, they are likely at an even greater disadvantage than even when the system was relatively stable—when they were already operating at a sizeable disadvantage (Galanter 1974; Shanahan, Carpenter, and Mark 2016). The present study sheds light on who has a say in shaping the processes that common court users encounter, which can inform conversations about how administrative procedure-making regimes can produce different experiences for those who access state civil courts.

Toward a Holistic View of State Court Administrative Decision-Making: Blending Perspectives from Judicial Politics and Judicial Administration

While this book narrows its focus to the processes that affect civil court operations and their users' experiences, it seeks to broaden our perspective on how we explain how courts work. The work of courts—and the study of that work—is largely undertaken by scholars who adhere to theoretical principles developed either within the judicial politics or judicial administration literature.[20] Within courts, adjudicatory and administrative efforts are complementary. Yet research on the choices courts make within these realms has largely become two separate enterprises. In this project, I make the case for a unified account of how courts make their administrative policies that leverages lessons from both literatures. From the judicial politics literature, the hierarchical model is particularly instructive. From the judicial administration literature, I borrow its conception of a more localized and diffuse account of decision-making. Considered together, these explanations help us understand the circumstances under which the formal administrative structure of courts constrains the independent policymaking efforts of court actors. Such an account, I argue, would offer a more holistic view of who participates in administrative policymaking in state courts.

Research on courts in political science largely focuses on the causes and consequences of adjudicative processes, whereas in judicial administration, it focuses more on the organizational features of courts that support their effective management. This split in the outcomes scholars seek to explain has also led to the development of contrasting theoretical approaches. When we think about how courts make adjudicatory decisions, we typically operate under a set of assumptions rooted in an institutional hierarchy. When we seek to explain administrative choices, we tend to look toward jurisdictions within states for explanations based in local context.

The hierarchical model assigns higher or lower levels of decisional autonomy to courts and judges according to the rung on the judiciary's ladder they find themselves. It relies on the premise that law develops through a system where judges evaluate the application and interpretation of rules given the circumstances in the case before them. Such a system hinges on something happening in a lower court that is capable of being monitored by a judge at a higher level through the appellate process (see, e.g., Boyd and Spriggs 2009; Randazzo 2008). This model is incredibly valuable for our understanding of how law develops and evolves through the review of case decisions. But the hierarchical model's relatively rigid vertical structure limits its utility as an explanation of the administrative choices that result from the types of decisions that court actors make outside of the courtroom.

State supreme courts do maintain control over the administration of the courts in their systems. This authority is constitutionally or statutorily vested in them, creating a hierarchical appearance in the administrative structures of courts. But unlike in the adjudicatory context, state supreme courts may lack the specific, practical tools necessary to effectively monitor and control the administrative decisions made by lower courts (see generally Boyd and Rutkowski 2020; see also Saari 1976; Gallas 1976; Schauffler 2007). It then follows that if supreme courts are vested with a general administrative power but exhibit variation in their specific ability to ensure that lower courts faithfully implement changes to process and operational guidelines, a hierarchical explanation of decision-making may not be sufficient as a stand-alone explanation of administrative decision-making behavior (see, e.g., Mark 2024).

An increasing number of scholars are drawing attention to the possibility that state courts' administrative governance structures may not be as hierarchical as previously assumed (e.g., Decker 2014; Weinstein-Tull 2020; Leib 2015; Carpenter et al. 2018; see also Bookman and Shanahan 2022). This literature theorizes about and empirically examines how state courts operate, exploring the regulations that enable different stakeholders to participate in civil procedure decision-making (e.g., Clopton 2018). These studies have involved detailed intrastate investigations that incorporate reviews of current rules and statutes, observations of in-court process modifications, and interviews with judges working in local courts. Through these projects, researchers have gained valuable insights into the administration of state courts and how individuals with civil justice issues experience the pathways that result from those courts' administrative policy decisions. Unlike the restrictions imposed on lower courts in the adjudicative hierarchy, this literature portrays lower courts as having some degree of flexibility in developing and implementing procedural policy. The concept of "administrative distance" from supreme courts and central administrative bodies may grant courts more leeway (Weinstein-Tull 2020,

1032). However, what remains unclear is how court actors differ in their actual and perceived "distance" based on the design of their judiciaries' administrative infrastructures.

I use these two literatures to structure my exploration of the distribution of procedural authority in state courts. Drawing from the hierarchical account, I argue that the distribution of a state court system's administrative powers will play a pivotal role in determining which actors within a system wield decision-making authority regarding the rules and processes that govern how their courts operate. More specifically, I argue that this variation will arise from the assignment of specific administrative responsibilities to actors within a court system. This differs from a blanket assumption that the general administrative authority vested in state supreme courts is determinative. State judiciaries vary in the extent to which these responsibilities are centrally managed, with the practical authority to direct procedure and court operations concentrated in varying degrees in the state's supreme court and statewide administrative office (Raftery 2015). In states with more centralized administration, lower courts will have very little in the way of formalized autonomy to independently design policy that fits their unique contexts. In states with more decentralized structures, local jurisdictions have considerably greater access to tools that would allow them to exercise control over local court operations, as the relationship between central management and courts is less adherent to a traditional hierarchical structure.

Due to variation in how state court systems are administered, I also argue that there is utility in incorporating a localized account of procedural authority. In addition to the structural features that affect the relationship between supreme and lower courts, courts and court actors vary in their relationship to their local institutional contexts. Lower courts situated in jurisdictions across a state may find themselves in contexts distinct from those within which individuals setting statewide policies operate (Leib 2015). Further, those working within state courts are not likely to have homogenous administrative preferences—their relationship to the courts in which they work is likely influenced by their own preferences and understandings of court operations (Boyd and Rutkowski 2020; see also Rosenberg 1971; Stott 1982). It thus follows that in addition to variation in formal permission or authorization to act, we would expect that courts staffed with people who *perceive* higher levels of latitude to act will be more likely to do so when their local contexts are in conflict with their high court's rule.

Leveraging elements from the hierarchical and the local accounts of adjudicatory and administrative decision-making, respectively, allows us to account for both the formal structure that determines who is assigned the authority to make policy and the individual behavioral determinants of performing that authority. In more administratively decentralized states where lower courts have more authority to take unilateral action, we may not observe much activity if the actors in the lower courts perceive compatibility with a high court's choices over court administration. In these jurisdictions, court actors will defer not because of requirement, but because they are aligned with those working at the top of the hierarchy. Conversely, in centralized states where lower courts are quite constrained by their hierarchal administrative structures, disagreement may spur actors working in these courts to take action, even in the face of monitoring or sanction. In these courts, the pull of their local context may weigh more heavily than these possible threats from above.

Unpacking Procedural Authority in State Court Systems: A Comparative Study

Scholars of the work of courts have paid attention to courts' procedural choices insofar as they contribute to explanations of the causes and consequences of decisions rendered through adjudication. Few studies have examined the relationship between state court systems' decisions on organizing administrative authority and how court actors interpret their role in making procedural and operational choices. Fewer still have endeavored to empirically investigate how these dynamics might vary across states. This book seeks to expand the way we think about administrative choices by using empirical evidence on the patterns of policy change undertaken during the COVID-19 pandemic. Importantly, and while acknowledging that the pandemic presented an unprecedented policy crisis for state courts across the country, the types of policy changes courts made were largely representative of procedural modifications that courts could have adopted under normal circumstances (e.g., Conference 2021, 2006 in Pew Charitable Trusts 2021). In fact, the vast majority of process-based changes that courts designed during the pandemic were being piloted or had otherwise been implemented in some number of jurisdictions across the country before the start of the pandemic (Pew Charitable Trusts 2021).

To study how court systems approach this form of policy-making, this book uses a multi-method empirical approach and relies on data from a series of novel data collection efforts. The first major data source is a comprehensive survey of all court orders, pieces of guidance, and other documents distributed by state courts in the first year of the pandemic. These documents represent those distributed across all levels of all state judiciaries in the United States and have been categorized and cataloged as such. This book principally relies on documents distributed by state supreme courts during this time period, and a digital companion to the book includes copies of all of the documents cited in text for quick reference. Additional data will also be made available via a user-friendly data dashboard, some uses of which are described in the conclusion of this book. This data dashboard represents an attempt to take an inclusive snapshot of all the formal activity undertaken by trial courts of general and limited jurisdiction, appellate courts, and system-level actors within each state court hierarchy. These documents were converted—either from pdfs or text files—into a corpus of searchable text that allows for both qualitative and quantitative analyses. This descriptive effort is meant, in part, to provide an organized archive of the flurry of activity undertaken in state courts during the first year of the pandemic across court levels.

In order to understand how the design and implementation of the aforementioned policies unfolded, the book also draws on personal interviews conducted with judges in administrative roles, trial and appellate court judges, court administrators (state, local), clerks, and other court staff between 2020 and 2022. These interviews explore how respondents participated in designing and implementing judicial responses to the pandemic, their perceptions of the attitudes of others working in their courts and court systems, the relationship between their court and other courts within and across levels of the hierarchy, and their views on the durability of innovations that their court may have implemented during the pandemic. The third data source is a novel collection of policy documents that relate to courts' consideration of permanent policy changes resulting from the pandemic experience through February 2023.

My analysis of the structural landscapes in state courts draws on literature from multiple disciplines, including political science, law, sociology, and public administration. Scholars in these fields have developed typologies to classify courts based on how they allocate authority for amending formal, systemwide rules and developing administrative policies (e.g., Clopton 2018; Raftery 2015; Henderson 1984). I rely on these typologies to introduce and describe the administrative functions of courts. Additionally, I gather information from states' civil procedure and systemwide court rules to supplement these typologies, as they provide insight into how local courts are empowered to create their own rules—a classification that is less prominent in the existing literature on court administration. I draw on these literatures and additional data sources to begin to identify indicators of how the formal allocation of administrative power in state courts is connected to the exercise of administrative policymaking authority. In addition, I speculate about the implications of these choices for individuals who rely on courts to resolve their legal disputes.

Theoretical, Empirical, and Practical Contributions of the Book

This book makes contributions of theoretical, empirical, and practical relevance. The project presents motivation for the development of a theoretical approach to understanding how court systems formulate and implement policies that govern their operations. Traditionally, the hierarchical model has shaped our understanding of how courts arrive at decisions, with higher courts setting policies that lower courts must adhere to. However, administrative power may be distributed more horizontally, with high courts possessing less authority in the administrative realm than they do in the adjudicatory realm. In such instances, the choices made by state supreme courts may be influenced by their degree of control over court operations. This challenges the application of a purely hierarchical perspective since supreme courts may not universally enjoy a concentrated source of authority in the administrative realm. Consequently, the incentives for lower courts to comply with supreme court policies may be limited, permitting them to diverge from high court preferences when they perceive it necessary.

In addition, this book aims to highlight the value of studying the activities of state courts that take place beyond the courtroom. While scholars examining the causes and consequences of choices made in court cases have acknowledged administrative decision-making, they have not typically explored it as the object of study. Rather, when researchers investigate these choices, they frequently utilize variations in the administrative policy landscape as indicators in models of adjudicatory patterns. This book contends that it is critical to examine the politics of courts' administrative policymaking since different administrative regimes can substantially affect court users' ability to obtain legal resolutions to their justice issues.

In terms of its empirical contributions, this book introduces an innovative dataset of court orders and describes a set of methods that could be used by scholars to conduct future analyses. One of the primary reasons why so few inter-state empirical studies of state courts exist is the challenges that arise in conducting such research. Public access to court data is extremely limited, not collected systematically across states, and collecting new data through observational methods requires significant time and effort (Carpenter et al. 2022a). However, these data, coupled with the analysis techniques demonstrated in this book, opens avenues for researchers to delve into the administrative aspects of court operations.

Beyond contributing to scholarly debates, this book also aims to be useful to courts and advocates interested in civil justice reform. First, the project provides a more comprehensive understanding of the role that the structure of administrative institutions plays in designing, implementing, and sustaining procedural change. This is a valuable insight, as it may influence approaches to advocating for changes to processes and operational policies in court systems, whether centralized or less centralized. It also prompts us to consider the utility of top-down and locally driven procedural change in various domains of court operations, sparking discussions about the types of decisions that are best managed at the state level versus those more effectively handled by individual jurisdictions. Both of these example areas offer perspectives that contribute to a conversation about the methods of procedural change—and the specific types of changes—that can improve the experiences and outcomes of people seeking resolutions to their civil legal problems using these institutions.

Plan of the Book

The following chapters explore the sources of power in state court systems and how they shape administrative policymaking, with a focus on the interplay between state supreme courts and lower courts' responses to the COVID-19 pandemic. Chapter 1 explores the various sources of power that courts have access to as they formulate the policies that govern court operations and case processing. The aim of this chapter is to provide a more nuanced understanding of the administrative policymaking landscape in court systems, highlighting variation in where power is concentrated within court systems to make these types of choices. To achieve this, it integrates perspectives on how high courts exercise authority in the adjudicatory context and in the administrative context. The chapter also provides an overview of the key sources of power that influence courts' administrative policymaking functions, which include statutory and constitutional provisions, civil procedure, court rules, and the assignment of control over specific administrative tools.

Chapter 2 examines the choices of state supreme courts during the COVID-19 pandemic, exploring the relationship between the centralization of administrative authority in state court systems and the language these courts used to promulgate policy changes. The chapter argues that state supreme courts are more likely to issue mandates or policies that require uniform implementation when they have the means to monitor or otherwise control the behavior of lower courts. The chapter presents an analysis of orders and guidance documents distributed by these institutions in the first four months of the pandemic to illustrate the differences in how state supreme courts guided procedural change. The chapter also proposes an alternative framework for studying state supreme courts' choices in the administrative realm, given the challenges of mapping court administrative centralization onto a single quantitative measure.

Chapter 3 builds on the previous chapter's argument about the relationship between the degree of centralization of a court system's administrative policy tools and a supreme court's performance of its administrative authority. This chapter offers an examination of how lower court actors responded to the policy choices of their supreme courts during the pandemic. More specifically, it explores the reasons why lower court actors might deviate from or comply with their supreme court's administrative preferences, taking into account structural factors and actors' perceptions of the alignment between their high courts' directives and their local contexts. The chapter draws from additional works in the public bureaucracy and administration literatures, applying explanations of compliance and defection to the supreme court/lower court relationship in the administrative sphere. It also presents an analysis of the policymaking activities in lower courts during the COVID-19 pandemic by leveraging a set of elite interviews in states where supreme courts have varying levels of control over administrative policy tools. Through this analysis, the chapter offers further evidence of how the hierarchical and local control models of judicial decision-making interrelate.

Chapter 4 shifts the focus of the book, turning to an examination of the implications of the temporary policy environment brought about by the pandemic for the permanent policies court systems chose to adopt for the post-pandemic period. Specifically, the chapter considers whether the intra-branch administrative power dynamics observed during the pandemic are unique or if they can also be applied to nonemergency contexts. The chapter compares the pandemic's emergency policymaking environment to the regular policymaking processes of state courts to determine whether the possession of administrative authority remains a stable feature of both decision-making contexts. I draw upon the findings of prior chapters and supplemental literature from the public policymaking and civil procedure-making literatures to provide insights about how central actors approach these processes under normal circumstances. The chapter uses a novel data collection of the proposed and codified changes to generally applicable bodies of rules across the states studied in chapter 2. It presents evidence indicating that control over administrative tools shapes the development of both temporary and permanent policies promulgated by supreme courts, contributing to the applicability of the argument advanced in chapter 2 across emergency and nonemergency contexts.

The concluding chapter charts a course for scholars interested in research extensions, specifically focusing on the avenues for future research that are relevant to developing a theory of the administrative work of state courts and to comprehending the shape of other temporary policies implemented during the pandemic. It also considers the implications of the findings on access to justice. This book represents an initial exploration of indicators pertinent to the administrative power dynamics of state courts. As such, I propose two additional studies utilizing indicators that, in my view, could contribute to shaping a comprehensive account of the hierarchical and local elements of administrative decision-making in court systems. I also present a series of empirical extensions, offering preliminary thoughts for further explorations of policy areas that were not the primary focus of this project. These proposed extensions focus both on the temporary pandemic context and the durability of policy choices as discussed in chapter 4. The chapter concludes by reflecting on the implications of the study for courts and civil justice advocates, emphasizing the need to consider both hierarchical dynamics and local influences in efforts to reform court processes, as well as to appreciate the impacts these structures and resulting choices have on people's access to justice.

1 | Navigating Administrative Power in State Court Systems
A Framework for Understanding Hierarchical and Local Influences

The power of courts to shape policy in common law systems, such as those in the United States, has long been associated with high courts or courts of last resort. This perspective is rooted in the concept of appellate power, which allows these courts to oversee and review the decisions made by lower courts and establish policies through their rulings that lower courts are generally bound to follow. However, this hierarchical model may not serve as a satisfactory explanatory tool for all policy decisions made by courts, including the administrative decisions that influence daily court operations and case processing. These administrative functions are structured differently across state court systems, leading to higher and lower concentrations of power at the state level. Thus, understanding who has the power to make administrative decisions challenges the traditional hierarchical model, as high court actors may not have access to similar monitoring mechanisms for this type of decision.

Scholars do not have a comprehensive understanding of how the distribution of administrative power in state court systems impacts the formulation and implementation of courts' operational policies. One reason for this may be that empirical scholars have had limited opportunities to comparatively study these dynamics. Researchers have primarily focused on either describing the administrative roles of lower court actors or examining their perceptions of their ability to create administrative policies that are tailored to their specific local contexts and goals (e.g., Weinstein-Tull 2020; Leib 2015). Such studies, while foundational, are limited in their ability to assess the interaction between hierarchical and local accounts of administrative power when developing explanations of who has the authority to devise and implement policies concerning case processing and court operations. However, we can infer from these studies that there are specific institutional structures that support a hierarchical model of authority, but that there is likely also variation in the extent to which high courts can access this formal power. It thus becomes necessary to investigate the sources of this variation in order to understand how it affects the power balance between high and lower courts in the administrative domain. This chapter aims to identify gaps in our understanding of administrative policymaking in court systems and prepare us for the empirical examination of administrative decision-making across court systems in subsequent chapters.

I begin by contrasting research on the exercise of authority by high courts in the adjudicatory context with that in the administrative context. I contend that while the hierarchical model may serve as a useful framework for understanding how lower courts should apply high courts' decisions in cases, it may not always be applicable to administrative decision-making due to the varied methods of distributing administrative authority. Therefore, additional considerations may need to be taken into account when applying the hierarchical model to administrative decision-making. To illustrate this variation in administrative authority, I then provide an overview of the institutions that guide the administration of court business, with particular attention paid to describing those that court actors have input in crafting and amending, such as civil procedure, generally and locally applicable court rules, and the guidelines that assign authority over different administrative tools, like information technology and budgetary decisions. This exercise shows that assessing the level of administrative centralization in a court system can be difficult due to the various sources of authority that can confer administrative power.

The Power to Make Policy in Court Systems

In the field of judicial politics, our understanding of how high courts transmit policy messages and why lower courts choose to comply with those messages is informed by a hierarchical model of decision-making that may not directly translate to the administrative context. The hierarchical model suggests that lower courts should follow the decisions of courts of last resort because these high courts can ensure compliance through the appellate process (e.g., Boyd and Spriggs 2009; Randazzo 2008). However, in the administrative context, there is a diverse range of organizational structures that do not necessarily mirror the top-down structure employed in courts' adjudicatory function (Raftery 2015; Weinstein-Tull 2020). In many areas of case processing and court operations policy, high courts may not have the same tools to exercise authority as they do in the adjudicatory space. In some cases, they may share these administrative powers with lower court actors or may lack authority altogether. Although high courts hold a position of authority within the adjudicatory hierarchy, we lack a comprehensive account of how a court system's administrative structure affects the communication of messages regarding operational policies by these bodies, and how these messages are interpreted by lower courts.

Scholars who study the determinants of these two types of policy choices (adjudicatory, administrative) that courts make are not typically in conversation with one another, and when they are, administrative choices are typically employed as indicators that help us understand adjudicatory choices as opposed to being explored as products of decision-making processes themselves. As one example, a body of scholarship considers the differences in the administrative pressures on trial and appellate judges as they work to develop the factual record or resolve questions of legal interpretation (see generally Kim et al. 2009). This scholarly split likely occurs because, perhaps quite obviously, scholars in these spaces are asking different types of questions of the decisions court actors make. As a consequence, they come to different conclusions about the goals of decision-making, what motivates those in positions of power to make the choices they make, and who has independence or is constrained in the exercise of their preferences.

The Appellate Power and Hierarchical Framework of Court Systems

The judicial decision-making literature in American politics is largely driven by a desire to explain the causes and consequences of judges' choices in the cases before them. This scholarship is informed by hierarchical understandings of how courts work—a top-heavy allocation of authority to high courts grants them the final say on branch-wide interpretations of law whereas the power of lower courts is limited by this structure (e.g., Boyd 2015; Boyd and Spriggs 2009; Randazzo 2008). However, judges and other court actors also make critical decisions about the administration of justice that affect court users' access to legal remedies (e.g., Kritzer 1982; Bazemore 1998, quoted in Johnson 2014; see also Yeazell 1994; Bone 2007). These decisions include those about how cases are initiated, documents are filed, hearings are scheduled and governed, and judgments are carried out, and they are often made outside of the adjudicatory framework.

When the judicial politics literature talks about judicial decision-making, the judiciary's hierarchical structure plays a key role in explanations of adjudicatory outcomes (or the results reached in cases). Scholars rely upon courts' hierarchical structures to explain why actors at the top of the hierarchy are relatively unhindered in achieving their policy goals while those below are constrained by the threat of monitoring through the appellate process (Songer, Segal, and Cameron 1994; Songer and Sheehan 1990; Benesh and Reddick 2002).[1] It is important to emphasize "threat" here—even if lower court actors' decisions do not have a high probability of being overturned by a higher court, they still tend to behave in a compliant fashion due to the possibility of such action (e.g., McNollgast 1995; Cameron 1993). The literature does not preclude the possibility of lower courts influencing policymaking by strategically shaping opinions to avoid reversal. Lower courts may do so to maintain local interpretations of the law or to provide guidance to appellate courts (e.g., Caldeira and Wright 1988; Lindquist and Klein 2006; Rachlinski 2006; Beim 2017; Savchak and Bowie 2016; Bowie and Savchak 2019). However, the hierarchy—and the formalized system of monitoring it relies on—creates a centralized system of power and functions as a structural limitation on the choices these courts make.

This literature does acknowledge that explaining the adjudicatory choices judges make requires an understanding of administrative policies that shape their institutional context. In particular, it recognizes that this context may vary according to the level of court. For example, scholars have advocated for the consideration of the myriad roles played by trial court judges as compared to appellate judges (e.g., case managers, settlement directors, developers of the factual record, jury wranglers) in studies of the choices they make in cases (see generally Kim et al. 2009; Resnik 1982; Bookman and Noll 2017). While these studies advocate for the consideration of the administrative work of judges, they do so in service of describing case processing within individual cases (Kim et al 2009, 89–90, 92). Put differently, these studies generally concentrate on incorporating the administrative features of courts into examinations of case outcomes rather than analyzing the factors that determine how these features come about.

Beyond Adjudicatory Contexts: Administrative Policy Choices in State Court Systems

While the hierarchical model is central to explaining how judges shape policy through case outcomes, it may not fully account for the types of choices courts make about how cases are processed and how they manage day-to-day operations outside of the adjudicatory context. As compared to the rigidity of the hierarchical structure of adjudicatory decision-making, court systems can differ in terms of who has a say in administrative decision-making according to how the authority to participate in such decisions is distributed within a court system. Recent studies have theorized about and empirically investigated this notion and have identified the informal and formal methods court actors use to affect administrative policy at the local and state levels. While studies have examined the authority of different state court actors to create administrative policies, these studies tend to be more limited in their scope and have focused on only certain types of authorities or specific jurisdictions (e.g., Weinstein-Tull 2020; Leib 2015). To fully understand the power dynamics within state courts' administrative systems, it is necessary to synthesize the findings from these studies and present a more comprehensive account of the sources of administrative authority that can be compared across different jurisdictions.

Although the empirical study of the authority to create administrative policies in state courts is still quite limited, it is recognized that judges and other court actors (e.g., clerks, court staff, court administrators) dedicate considerable time to crafting these types of policies (Ryan et al. 1980; Smith and Feldman 2001; Clopton 2018; Hershkoff 2001; Bookman and Shanahan 2022; see generally Carpenter et al. 2022b; but see Pollack 2021, 719, 724, 730–758). There have been important scholarly advancements in this area, but many contemporary works concentrate on the development of informal processes within specific courts (for a review of the literature, see Carpenter et al. 2022a). In essence, these studies analyze how courts make unofficial procedural adjustments, often in an opaque and ad hoc manner, based on their particular circumstances (Sudeall and Pasciuti 2021, 1365, 1379; Shanahan et al. 2020; Carpenter et al. 2018; see also Bookman and Shanahan 2022; Bookman and Noll 2017). Those that focus on formal authority have mapped the different channels through which supreme courts can affect their systems' administrative policies, such as through the making of generally applicable civil procedure at the state level (e.g., Clopton 2018; see also Reinhart and Coppolo 2002). They have also described the allocation of various practical administrative powers across levels of court administration (e.g., Raftery 2013, 2015; see also Henderson 1984).

Scholars have also, in a limited empirical scope, analyzed

local courts' reactions to policy regimes in court systems with more (or less) centralized administrative structures (e.g., Weinstein-Tull 2020; Leib 2015). These studies tend to downplay a hierarchical view of administrative power, offering evidence that suggests central administrative actors have relinquished control to lower courts in various administrative spaces over time (Weinstein-Tull 2020, 1066–1067). Yet even when state-level actors hold significant authority over court operations decisions, the complex organizational structures of state courts can lead to inadequate monitoring of choices that disregard or deviate from a state supreme court's mandate. In other words, even in systems with more centralized administrative structures, high courts and central administrators are still limited in their ability to police such deviations (Weinstein-Tull 2020, 1102; see also Leonetti 2012). As a consequence, scholars argue that supreme courts may not be able to entirely rely on their position at the top of the hierarchy as deterministic of the branch-wide implementation of their preferences over case processing and court operations.

Studies of the allocation of administrative power in state courts have advanced more and less hierarchical accounts of this authority, but have done so in ways that either consider one category or type of authority (e.g., the power to make state-level civil procedure, the allocation of practical administrative power) or multiple types of authorities as they pertain to the administrative governance of single jurisdictions (e.g., the study of one state or a set of lower courts within a state). If we are to look across jurisdictions to categorize state courts' administrative apparatuses as more or less hierarchical in their design, it is important to establish the ways in which court actors vary in their ability to participate in making the different categories of rules and operational choices that guide administrative policy in their systems.

The Administrative Power Structure in State Court Systems

Although state supreme courts are typically vested with the authority to oversee the administration of their branches via constitutional and statutory provisions, there is significant variation in how that general grant of power is put into practice.[2] Multiple bodies of rules govern the processing of court cases and the management of daily court operations that support various aspects of court business. These rules, including constitutional and statutory provisions, civil procedure rules, local and generally applicable court rules, and the guidelines that govern the assignment of administrative and operational responsibilities, vary in the extent to which they concentrate authority in state supreme courts and other central policymaking bodies in court systems. While constitutional and statutory provisions are important determinants of the shape of courts' administrative power, this section principally focuses on identifying the key rule categories, practical administrative tasks, and operational powers that court actors are most commonly involved in designing, managing, and implementing. The allocation of the power to make policies in these categories can vary across state court systems, resulting in a diversity of administrative organizational styles that may be more or less hierarchical in their orientation.

Statutory and Constitutional Obligations

At the top of the hierarchy of rules that shape court operations are the substantive statutory and constitutional obligations of courts to parties involved in legal disputes. While supreme courts and court systems may attempt to modify these obligations by making appeals to the legislature (e.g., via requests made in annual reports) or through handing down decisions that prompt a legislative response, these rules generally create durable expectations that shape the court processes and procedures that are designed to uphold them. The extent to which statutory and constitutional obligations address the specific methods by which courts can fulfill their duties to parties can vary. Consequently, each state court system is responsible for developing a distinctive set of processes and operational guidance that is meant to effectively implement these provisions in their respective jurisdictions.

The pandemic experience offers an example of how the power to design processes and operations can be shaped by constitutional and statutory obligations. Although this project primarily concerns the procedural choices affecting the civil legal system, the right to a speedy trial provides a straightforward example of how courts use their administrative powers to carry out their obligations to parties. Choices of this sort are also relevant to the processing of civil cases: the obligations that I describe below influenced the prioritization of criminal cases as well as certain categories of civil cases over others during the pandemic.

The requirement for a speedy criminal trial is guaranteed by the Bill of Rights in the US Constitution and in forty-one state-level constitutions, as well as via federal law through the Speedy Trial Act of 1974 and similar state laws. However, the specificity of these requirements as they are codified into substantive state law varies considerably. In general, statutory provisions are more specific than constitutional guarantees. Most states set maximum time limits for different stages of criminal case processing, but some states rely on language similar to their constitutional guarantees instead of establishing explicit time limits.[3] For example, while Illinois law maintains a 120-day or 160-day standard for a speedy trial for defendants in custody or on bail, respectively, Tennessee and Utah law codifies the right to a speedy trial in statute with no mention of a time standard.[4] Delaware lacks a statutory right to a speedy trial but maintains the right to a speedy trial in its state constitution with no codified time standard.[5] These varied approaches to the language of obligation require courts to develop different sets of rules in order to meet those statutory and constitutional requirements.

During the pandemic, fulfilling speedy trial obligations required court systems to make operational decisions across different types of cases, prioritizing categories of hearings and court actions where these obligations were most pressing, while deprioritizing others.[6] Public health concerns posed a threat to courts' ability to meet these obligations as other operational challenges posed by the pandemic, like bringing prospective jurors and witnesses to court, were complicated by stay-at-home orders and social distancing requirements. In response, in states where supreme courts promulgate procedural changes, high courts used their authority to craft temporary procedural responses to these challenges. Some state supreme courts, like Illinois's, interpreted its procedural authority with respect to the speedy trial requirement to allow for its relaxation in the early days of the pandemic.[7] Other states, like Utah, experimented with alternative procedures incorporating public health measures in order to continue to hold trials in order to meet obligations to parties in spite of a lack of time requirements codified in statute.[8] Across states, courts used their administrative powers to balance the interests of the state with the rights of defendants while also considering broader public health considerations when designing their operational policies.

Procedure and Generally Applicable Court Rules

As evidenced in the previous section, the ways in which statutory and constitutional provisions are implemented through procedural choices can vary depending on the degree of specificity with which these obligations are codified and a court's interpretation of what it means to faithfully carry them out. It can also vary according to the degree of independent authority that is delegated to courts to make these determinations. Rules about case processing attempt to comprehensively map out what is required of parties and attorneys at each stage of the trial process across all courts in a given judicial system (Avraham and Hubbard 2022; Marcus 2013). At the case initiation phase, this includes rules about filing complaints and issuing summonses. In the pre-trial and trial phases, formal procedure maps out requirements related to defining the interested parties and the scope of discovery, requests for trial by jury, and conditions for dismissal of a case. At the post-trial phase, it includes rules about judgments and provisional and final remedies. These rules also explain how court systems are to go about establishing specialty courts and policies to govern them. Even though most states have adopted the general contours of the procedural rules used by the federal judiciary, many also exercise their independent authority to make modifications and otherwise differentiate themselves from the federal courts' rules (Clopton 2018).[9]

The authority to design and approve of modifications to code- or rule-based procedure is typically vested in central bodies responsible for judicial policymaking within a state, and states vary according to the types of actors who get to participate in the decision-making process. In some states, like California, Illinois, and New York, procedure is primarily promulgated via legislative action.[10] However, it is more common for these rules to be established internally by state supreme courts based on power extended to them by constitutional and/or statutory provisions, or on a court's interpretation of its inherent authority to do so. In some of these states, the legislature maintains some degree of control over the outputs of these processes and can veto or make amendments to the procedural changes supreme courts advance. It is more common, however, for a legislature to make a statutory enactment to which courts must respond than it is for it to disapprove of a court's proposed change.[11]

The body of civil procedure resulting from these formal processes presents opportunities for courts to issue rules and construct operational guidelines that facilitate its implementation. Procedure is meant to be, in large part, broadly applicable across areas of law, remedies sought, and parties involved.[12] This universality comes with its merits—it ensures that the same procedural protections are available to everyone who uses the legal system or who interacts with one specific area of law (Reda 2017; but see Coleman 2018).[13] However, the level of generality creates policy problems for courts and those working within them: producing general procedures meant for all circumstances means that some level of detail will be lost, leaving state, jurisdiction, and often individual court-level policymakers to fill in gaps, clarify, or otherwise interpret procedure in order to apply it in their contexts (see generally Carpenter et al. 2018, 2022b; Bookman and Noll 2017; Bookman and Shanahan 2022).

Court Rules and Operational Guidelines

The level of authority granted to actors outside of supreme courts and other central decision-making bodies to contribute to the creation of policies and guidelines that support generally applicable procedural choices varies from one court system to another. Picking up the case prioritization example here is instructive. State supreme courts developed generally applicable, temporary case prioritization schemes relevant to their obligations to criminal defendants and those involved in civil cases with a safety concern early in the pandemic. These case prioritization determinations applied to all courts in these systems, but in some systems, the opportunity for local-level variation was introduced as court capacity increased. Some supreme courts granted their lower courts the ability to make locally applicable determinations about other types of cases that could be considered priorities, and as courts built out their virtual infrastructures, some supreme courts also permitted lower courts to make determinations about which initially deprioritized cases they would begin to hear again, like those involving small claims and other money damages cases, disputes arising in family and housing law that did not involve a public safety concern, and probate cases.[14]

Local rules and guidelines are examples of policies that can serve to modify or explain generally applicable procedure and support courts' operations and core functions given local conditions. Even though this type of authority is not always apportioned with clear boundaries within court systems, we can examine both the rules that govern the making of locally applicable court rules and scholars' attempts to describe and quantify the distribution of operational authority to get some sense of the various ways court systems formally assign the capacity to make decisions in these areas.

LOCAL COURT RULES

Local court rules are crafted to fill the breach, whether implicit or explicit, that is created by generally applicable sets of rules

like civil procedure and other statewide policies issued by supreme courts. Since civil procedure and other statewide rules
need to be broad in their construction, local courts seek to design and implement various policies to fill gaps they have identified. Local rulemaking enables lower courts to craft policies that
offer guidance and additional details on how to comply with the
general framework established by these statewide rules while addressing the needs of the local context. However, the degree to
which statewide systems of rules codify permissions to establish
local court rules varies, resulting in the potential for inconsistent interpretations of procedure both within and across court
systems (Levin 1991). Some systems afford their lower courts
more opportunities to come up with innovative solutions to fill
gaps in procedure, while others may have fewer opportunities
to do so.

A review of the guidelines for local rulemaking in state court
systems, as outlined in their uniform rules and statutes, reveals
that there are various procedures and court actors involved in
creating court rules that are applicable at the local level. This
diversity in processes and participants is similar to what was observed in Clopton's (2018) landmark empirical study of the procedures for amending civil procedure at the state level. State
courts' local rulemaking procedures typically fall into one of
three categories: systems are either broadly permissive of local
rulemaking, permissive with a preference for uniformity, or actively discourage local rules in favor of uniformity. The degree
of permissiveness tends to be influenced by the competing val-
ues of uniform application of procedure and responsiveness to
a court's local context. In states that preferred uniform application, the structure of the rule approval process reflected that
value.

The majority of states are broadly permissive of the making
of locally applicable rules governing court processes. Court
systems with permissive local rulemaking processes tended
to define local rules and lay out the process from proposal to
promulgation in ways that were very similar to that described in
the Federal Rules of Civil Procedure.[15] Where permissive states
tended to differ from the federal rules was in the actors involved

Local Rule Style

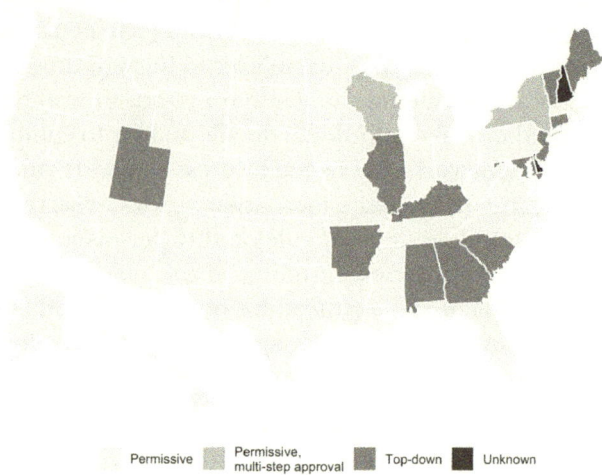

Figure 1.1. Differences in the permissibility of local rulemaking authority within state court guidelines
Source: State-level local rulemaking definition and procedures, on file with author.

in the rulemaking process: in the federal system, local rules are reviewed and adopted through a process internal to the given district court. Although many state systems included a vote of the given lower court's judges in their approval processes, it was much more common for other actors to be involved in addition to this group. State supreme courts were the most common authorizing body across states in this group.

In states that were more restrictive of the promulgation of local rules, it was (not surprisingly) rare to observe the use of the federal system's description of local rules or the process prescribed by the rule to approve of them. In several of these states, a version of the more permissive federal rule had previously been on the books but the state's supreme court had since taken steps to abolish it, often replacing it with a supreme court rule that articulated a process that was more supportive of uniform court rules. In a few states, the local court rulemaking process allowed for the creation of local rules while simultaneously trying to prevent an excessive number of locally applicable rules from being made. In Utah, for example, the process for approving local rules includes a review of a proposed rule's "potential application to courts of equal jurisdiction and its potential application to all courts of record and not of record."[16] Virginia takes a similar approach.[17] When Indiana modified its procedures for local rulemaking in 2007, it mandated that all trial courts within a county adopt a single set of rules but allowed for internal variation in these sets given "geographic, jurisdictional, and other variables."[18]

A final group of states utilize an approach to local rulemaking that provides for a greater level of state actor control over lower courts' choices. Some court systems in this group permitted the promulgation of local rules for a narrow band of activity. For example, while Georgia and Illinois articulate a preference for statewide applications of rules in their guidance for creating local rules, both states permit forms of local rulemaking that governs what Georgia's rules for its municipal and superior courts refer to as "internal processes."[19] In Georgia, lower courts are able to "maintain practices and standing orders . . . in matters which are not susceptible to uniformity."[20] In Illinois, lower courts are permitted to "make rules regulating their dockets, calendars, and business."[21] Similarly, Arkansas engaged in a reconsideration of its system of local rules in the late 1980s, and reasoned that the inconveniences and potential for miscarriages of justice in a system full of local rules outweighed any "inconvenience caused by not having local rules."[22] In Arkansas, however, trial courts are permitted to enter administrative orders that "attend to necessary housekeeping measures."[23]

The level of autonomy granted to local courts in creating rules that apply within their jurisdiction varies from state to state. While some states' rules offer greater flexibility to lower courts as long as their local rules adhere to statewide guidelines, others impose more constraints and have developed mechanisms to review the impact of proposed local rules on the state level. This divergence in procedures leads to unequal opportunities for lower courts to propose creative solutions to issues.[24] It is important to consider this procedural variation when assessing the ability of lower courts to devise responsive procedures that address local contexts.

OPERATIONAL GUIDELINES AND ADMINISTRATIVE RESPONSIBILITIES

The guidelines that structure the day-to-day operations of courts intersect with systemwide and local rules and processes. Operational guidance represents the choices courts make about how they function, which are in the service of case processing and other features of their work (Tobin 1997; Aikman 2006).[25] These policies are not necessarily in direct conversation with formal procedures and rules, but they are essential for courts to carry out their core functions. Scholars have attempted to measure court systems' assignment of operational authority in various ways, but the concept is challenging to accurately measure.[26] The NCSC's State Court Organization (SCO) survey is a notable comprehensive effort that focuses on measuring the level of control state court administrators report having over various operational functions of court systems.[27] The survey provides a way to quantify the level of control that central actors possess, making it a useful tool for those interested in understanding the dynamics of administrative power in court systems.

The results of this survey have been applied to analyses of the relationship between the diffusion of administrative authority and court efficiency (e.g., Raftery 2015) and in descriptions of local court power (e.g., Weinstein-Tull 2020). The contents of the survey have changed somewhat over time, and states vary in their participation—making it difficult to make longitudinal comparisons. The 2016 iteration of the survey is most pertinent to this analysis, as it is the most recent version that asked state court administrators to report on a number of questions related to facilities management, budgeting, administrative and technical assistance, legal support, public and governmental relations, and judicial selection and evaluation—most categories of which help us understand how much control local and state-level actors have over court operations.[28] Specifically, in the 2016 iteration of the survey, state court administrators were asked if central

Table 1.1. Categories of Responsibilities Assigned to State- and Local-Level Administrative Bodies

Category	Specific Activities Reported
Judicial selection and evaluation	Appointment of sitting judges, appointment of supplemental judges, performance measurement, judicial education, judicial performance
Information system and technical support services	Records management, data processing, information technology, technical assistance
Building management	Facilities management, facilities security
Court services	Court-annexed ADR, emergency management, foster care review, adult and juvenile probation, law library staff
Legal services	General counsel, other legal services
Public and governmental relations	Liaison to legislature, liaison to ombudsman, liaison to public information
Research activities	Court statistics, research/planning, legal research staff
Financial and budgetary services	Collection of legal financial obligations, accounting, audits, budget preparation, purchasing
Court personnel management (staff)	Human resources

Source: NCSC Court Statistics Project, State Court Organization survey (2016), data archived by Weinstein-Tull (2020).

offices had total, shared (with lower courts), or no control over operations in thirty-one specific policy subcategories, which can be found in table 1.1.[29] Although self-reporting comes with its disadvantages, the data collected by the NCSC represents the most comprehensive collection of this type of information about state courts, with forty-two states and the District of Columbia responding during the survey's 2016 administration period.[30]

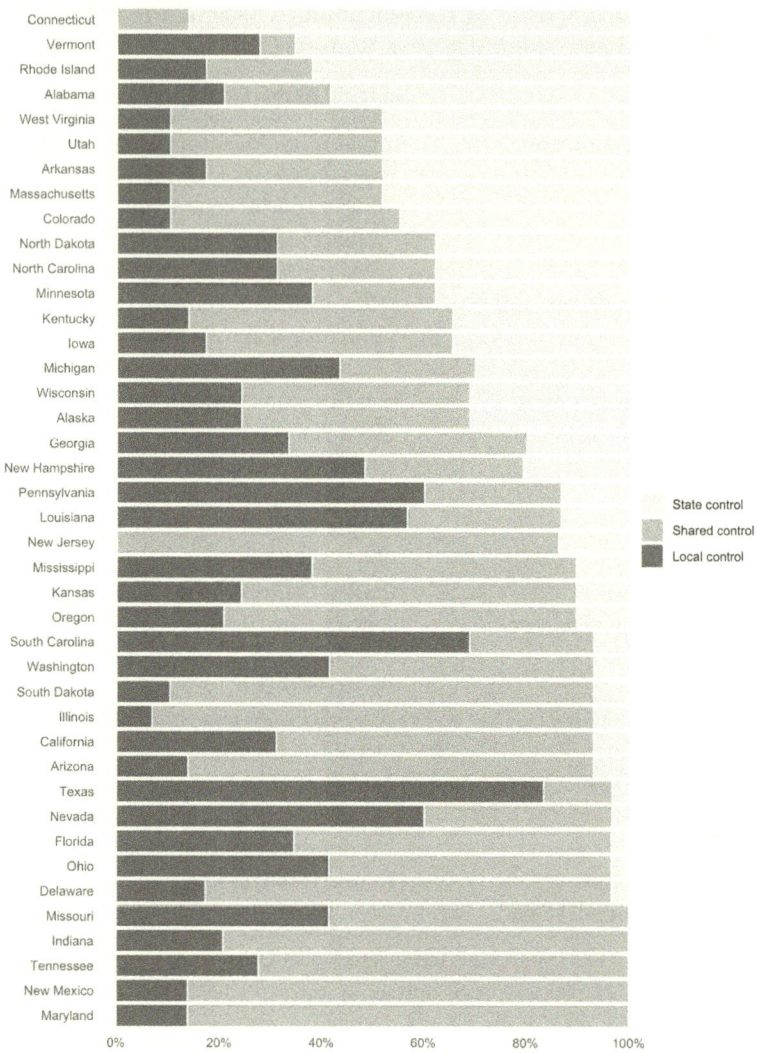

Figure 1.2. Reported level of state-level administrators' control over operations-related decision-making, ordered by state-level control
Source: NCSC Court Statistics Project, State Court Administrators survey (2016), data archived by Weinstein-Tull (2020).

As demonstrated in figure 1.2, authority over the features of court operations is reported to be allocated in forty-three different combinations—no two states (nor the District of Columbia) are exactly alike. The judiciaries that assert statewide control over the greatest number of the administrative areas mentioned in table 1.1 are Connecticut (86% of policy areas), Vermont (65%), Rhode Island (62%), and Alabama and Hawai`i (each at 58%). Across these five states, shared control between state-level and local administrators is slightly more likely than complete local control of an area. Shared control was most common in areas that affected courts' physical locations and their operations, including facilities management (Vermont, Alabama, Hawai`i), facilities security (Alabama, Hawai`i), collection of fines and fees (Rhode Island, Alabama), and data processing (Rhode Island, Alabama). Local control was most common in areas where local courts have substantive legal responsibilities: adult probation (all but Connecticut), juvenile probation (Vermont, Rhode Island, Hawai`i), foster care review (all but Connecticut), and in the management of court-annexed alternative dispute resolution (ADR) (Rhode Island, Alabama).

In seven states, administrators reported that there were no policy areas over which state actors exerted total control (Texas, Nevada, Missouri, Tennessee, Indiana, Maryland, New Mexico). In this group of states, we do see variation in the level of shared policy authority. In Indiana, Maryland, New Mexico, and Tennessee, administrators reported that they shared policy authority with lower court administrators over a majority of policy areas. Conversely, local court administrators in Texas and Nevada have considerably more authority than the statewide administrative office, with the local level controlling 86 percent and 62 percent, respectively, of the policy areas. Not unlike the states where total control was most likely, the majority of the locally controlled states also tended to have authority over substantive legal responsibilities like ADR (Texas, Nevada, Missouri, Tennessee, Indiana), adult probation (Texas, Nevada, Missouri, Tennessee, Maryland, New Mexico), juvenile probation (Texas, Nevada, Tennessee, Maryland, New Mexico), and foster care review (Texas, Nevada, Missouri, New Mexico). The most common shared responsibilities included those concerning information technology and court statistics, with all states reporting shared governance of these areas. All but Texas and all but Nevada shared responsibility in the areas of performance measurement and research/planning, respectively.

In most states, state-level administrators reported exerting control over at least some areas of administrative policymaking, but across states only judicial education is most commonly considered a state-level matter (53% of states). While technical assistance, court statistics, and research and planning are also highly likely to be controlled by state-level judicial officers, it is more common that these three responsibilities are shared between state and local administrators. State court administrators have the least authority over substantive legal responsibilities like ADR. It is also somewhat common for trial courts to have full control over the management and security of their facilities, as well as over the measurement of judicial performance.

The distribution of practical administrative authority creates variation in the ability of court systems and individual courts to create and enforce general and local forms of rules and policies. When local courts have control over domains such as information technology, budgeting, or building management, there may be a greater potential for diversity in implementing procedures and rules, as opposed to when those domains are managed by high courts. Returning to the example of case prioritization, during the pandemic some state supreme courts offered lower courts the discretion to expand the types of cases they could hear as the effects of the pandemic were better understood. In states where lower courts had control over operational tools related to their capacity to take on more cases, variations in decisions about caseload thresholds and case types that could be scheduled for hearings may have arisen according to a court's local context. In other words, because court systems differ in the ways they approach the distribution of administrative authority, some offer more opportunities to tailor operational policies to local contexts than others.

Toward a More Nuanced Understanding of Administrative Power in Court Systems

State courts exhibit diverse administrative organizational structures. Although state supreme courts are granted a general form of authority to administer their branches via constitutional and statutory provisions, when creating generally applicable rules and processes, some judiciaries possess complete authority to design and establish procedural changes, while others share that power with their legislatures. In developing rules that may not be generally applicable, state judiciaries offer varying levels of autonomy to lower courts to formalize their own local rules. Additionally, state-level administrative bodies may exercise full control over the majority of decisions regarding operational guidelines, or lower courts may have greater influence over managing their operations than their judiciary's central administrative body.

Identifying where decisional authority lies enables us to consider it when explaining the administrative policies that courts formulate to guide their operations. However, the complex procedural and operational landscape, along with the diversity of actors who participate in policy design, makes it difficult to categorize state judiciaries based on their level of administrative centralization. Despite lacking a definitive method for classifying courts, understanding how states formally allocate these authorities provides a structural framework for anticipating how courts make administrative policy decisions.

The following chapter considers how state court systems' adherence to or deviations from a hierarchical administrative structure influences high courts' policy decisions concerning court operations and case processing. I leverage works from the public bureaucracy literature to develop expectations about the types of administrative policies we would expect a high court to promulgate in the presence or absence of the tools necessary to ensure lower court compliance with its choices. Using the variations in the distribution of administrative power identified in this chapter as a foundation for this analysis, I will argue that differences in the features of administrative policy choices made by supreme courts are influenced by the capacity of high courts and central administrators to contribute to the faithful implementation of the supreme court's decisions.

2 | Linking Administrative Capacity and State Supreme Courts' Policy Choices during the Pandemic

In the previous chapter I discussed the sources of variation in the control that state supreme courts and central administrators have over rulemaking processes and the development of operational guidelines that regulate administrative functions within their systems. I illustrated this by providing a brief overview of the key forms of variation in the processes underlying the creation of civil procedure and other generally and locally applicable bodies of rules, as well as the allocation of authority over specific administrative policymaking domains. In this chapter I delve into the implications of these varying levels of authority by exploring the policies implemented by state supreme courts during the COVID-19 pandemic.

The onset of the COVID-19 pandemic posed significant challenges for state court leaders across the United States, as they had to make crucial decisions regarding the day-to-day operations of their respective court systems. Some leaders adopted an approach that provided individual jurisdictions with the flexibility to experiment with diverse procedural methods tailored to meet the specific needs of their communities. Meanwhile, others adopted a more centralized approach, retaining greater control over the modification of procedures and offering lower courts a more structured set of options for processing civil cases during the public health emergency.

Our understanding of the mechanisms that underlie state supreme courts' direction of procedure and court operations is limited, making it difficult to explain the variations in their approaches to crafting policy responses to the pandemic. The complex nature of the relationship between their constitutional powers and the practical tools at their disposal further contributes to the challenge. As described in the previous chapter, scholars have mapped the formal channels through which supreme courts can affect their systems' administrative policies (e.g., Clopton 2018; see also Raftery 2015). Scholars have also, in a limited empirical scope, analyzed local courts' reactions to policy regimes in court systems with more (less) centralized administrative structures (e.g., Weinstein-Tull 2020; Leib 2015). Prior to the onset of the COVID-19 pandemic, we had not had an opportunity to see these formal pathways employed to address a distinct policy challenge at such a substantial scale.

This chapter builds upon the structural variations in state court systems' administrative arms as described in the previous chapter. It examines the connection between distinct distributions of administrative power and the policy language used by top administrative actors. To accomplish this, the study draws on scholarship from the public bureaucracy and administrative law fields, which provide valuable insights on how power functions within complex organizations such as court systems. The chapter then applies the ways in which formal authority is implemented in organizations through different policy instruments to the judicial context. It argues that state supreme courts are more likely to issue mandates or policies that require uniform implementation when they have the means to monitor or otherwise control the behavior of lower courts. To illustrate the differences in how state supreme courts guided procedural change during the COVID-19 pandemic, the chapter presents an analysis of orders and guidance documents distributed by these institutions in the first four months of the pandemic. The chapter also acknowledges the challenges of mapping court administrative centralization onto a single quantitative measure and proposes an alternative framework for studying state supreme courts' choices in the administrative realm.

The Interplay of Hierarchical and Local Influences on High Courts' Administrative Policymaking

The hierarchical model, which outlines one perspective on how courts communicate policy messages and enforce lower court compliance, may not always be applicable in the administrative context. This is because there are different organizational structures that may not facilitate the use of a top-down approach. The hierarchy of courts is central to explanations of how judges make policy through case outcomes, but this model may not produce a comprehensive explanation of decision-making outside of the courtroom. While scholars have directed the field's attention to variation in administrative power structures in state courts in recent years, particularly to the fact that state supreme courts may have limited control over administrative functions, they have yet to fully consider how hierarchical and local influences shape high courts' administrative policymaking decisions. Therefore, the question remains: how does the extent of a state supreme court's practical administrative power relate to its expression of preferences on matters concerning case processing and court operations?

In the administrative context, the tools central actors have to both convey their preferences and compel compliance may be quite different from those they enjoy when they act in their adjudicative function. Borrowing terminology from the administrative law and public bureaucracy literatures, high courts may instead have a variety of binding and nonbinding policy tools at their disposal (see, e.g., Vedung 1998; Guzman and Meyer 2010).

Binding policies are available to high courts that wield authority over a given policy domain: if they control an area in a practical sense, they should be able to craft policy that constrains lower courts' independent deviations from their preferred policies. However, high courts can also use nonbinding policy tools—recommendations that nudge lower courts toward their preferences without the backing of strict enforcement mechanisms. State supreme courts in centralized and less centralized systems alike might favor nonbinding tools either because they do not have the ability to ensure compliance or because they may see them as easier to promulgate. Both explanations are pertinent to the policy dilemmas courts faced during the pandemic.

In states where administrative power is highly centralized, supreme courts and state-level administrators may be able to construct binding forms of policies about case processing as they have access to mechanisms that help to enforce compliant behavior (Behn 2001; Gormley and Balla 2004; Thierer 2021). Conversely, where local courts have independent authority in administrative policy domains, state-level actors may not have tools at their disposal to enforce their preferred policies. Under these circumstances, state-level actors may be more likely to resort to developing nonbinding policies, or those "governance mechanisms that lack the same degree of enforceability" of binding policies (Thierer 2021, 80; Snyder 1994; see also Bardach and Kagan 1982). These policies are considered lawlike in nature but do not have the same ability to compel behavior as a binding policy. Instead, they may provide implementing populations with cues about the policymaker's preferences over a course of action through the provision of recommendations, guidance, and clarification (see generally Snyder 1994; Anthony 1992).

The use of recommendations and guidance to convey a policy actor's preferred course of action is not an uncommon tactic in American politics. For example, bureaucratic agencies often rely on the provision of guidance as a vehicle for communicating their preferences for how the entities they regulate should behave. This guidance may come in a variety of forms, including white papers and reports, documents that advance best practices, and voluntary "opt-in" regulatory pilot projects (see Sandefur and Denne 2022). Guidance is distinct from an agency's formally promulgated rules as it is meant to serve an advisory function for the targeted entities. Even so, scholars have identified that such policy documents can have practical effects (Senden 2004, 112, in Cappellina et al. 2022) on the observable behaviors of those to whom the guidance is targeted.

Efficiency of adoption and ease of amendment are key reasons scholars cite as to why administrative agencies might express their policy preferences through nonbinding means. Of course, there are rules that dictate how these guidance documents are constructed, approved of, and distributed (e.g., in the federal case, the Administrative Procedure Act offers such rules; see also Parrillo 2019; Potts 2021). But it is often simpler and more efficient to disseminate policies using these types of mechanisms as compared to the processes that lead to the production of formal rules. This efficiency differential is of particular relevance in an emergency situation like that presented by the pandemic (Stefan 2020). Due to the relative procedural simplicity associated with disseminating advisory forms of policy as compared to making changes to formal rules, even those actors with high levels of control over the administration of their court systems are likely to see the value in the ability to rapidly respond with nonbinding tools.

In addition to the speed at which preferences can be promoted using guidance, state supreme courts may opt to offer suggestions for policy change because they lack the authority to compel behavior or otherwise enforce their proposed policy choices. We can continue to draw upon the bureaucratic analog with respect to this explanation: agencies may produce formal rules in the spaces that they are statutorily empowered to do so and generate guidance in the areas that they are not. For example, in 2000 the Department of Health and Human Services (HHS) delegated to the Centers for Disease Control and Prevention (CDC)—a public health agency under its authority—the power to craft binding interstate and foreign quarantine regulations (previously, this authority was split between the CDC and FDA over foreign and interstate quarantine measures, respectively). Such regulatory authority is granted to the HHS by statute, and the HHS exercises its ability to "make and enforce such regulations [that are necessary to] prevent the introduction, transmission, and spread of communicable diseases" via the CDC (42 US § 264 in Shen 2021). This power to design and implement quarantine regulations led the CDC to impose a number of measures during the first year of the COVID-19 pandemic, including quarantine, virus testing, and medical reporting requirements for overseas air travelers and a nearly yearlong nationwide freeze on residential evictions (e.g., Benfer et al. 2022).

These measures were, in large part, determined to be appropriate exercises of the CDC's authority under the Public Health Service Act. But there were other areas of pandemic containment over which the CDC had established preferences but could not compel behavior due to the limitations of its statutory authority.[1] For example, the CDC is limited in its ability to impose a nationwide vaccine mandate, as such regulations—when they have been necessary—have historically been the purview of states and localities. Given this limitation, the CDC instead opted to disseminate a significant amount of guidance that promoted a recommended COVID-19 vaccination schedule for both school-age children and adults (CDC, "COVID-19 Vaccination for Children"). Contrasting these examples—the authority to compel behavior in the case of quarantines and the dissemination of vaccination guidance in the absence of such authority—demonstrates how the boundaries of an institution's authority structure its approach to advancing solutions to policy problems.[2]

The administrative law and public bureaucracy literatures provide a framework for understanding how administrators in high-level positions interpret and carry out their roles through the policies they choose to disseminate. Administrators have access to a range of policy tools that they can use depending on their capacity to ensure compliance among those they regulate. While administrators with significant enforcement power may prefer to use binding tools to compel or incentivize adherence, nonbinding recommendations and guidance can effectively disseminate policies across diverse organizational structures. Guidance can be used flexibly, allowing regulators to experiment with different implementation approaches for targeted groups. It can promote a shared understanding of the course of action and encourage behavior change among those who see it as trustworthy and legitimate. Courts, acting in their administrative capacities, may also find value in producing guidance that complements enforceable policies and expands on the language used in binding rules. Therefore, guidance can be a valuable policy tool for court systems with both strong and weak centralized administrative structures whereas binding tools are more likely to be used by administrators with a high level of authority in a given policy space.

Measuring Administrative Power over the Use of Technology in Court Systems

During the first year of the pandemic, state supreme courts and state-level administrative offices issued a significant amount of policy documents with provisions meant to support the continuity of court operations. The way they chose to convey the policy messages these documents contained varied in important ways.[3] In some cases, like that of case prioritization described in the previous chapter, state supreme courts relied on the constitutional and statutory obligations of courts to litigants to justify the mandates they promulgated with respect to the prioritization of certain types of hearings in the early days of the pandemic. We also observed in the case prioritization example variation in how strictly state supreme courts defined the boundaries of what was prioritized: in some states, supreme courts delegated a considerable amount of authority to lower courts to determine what additional case types could be deemed a priority.[4]

Although the scholarly literature demonstrates a connection between the use of policies that do or do not bind regulated entities according to both efficiency and authority rationales, we lack a good understanding of how these different approaches to policymaking manifest within court systems and across categories of administrative authority. To examine this relationship, I consider the policy language supreme courts promulgated that related to the transition to the remote environment during the first four months in which courts disseminated pandemic-related orders, or March 2020 through the end of June 2020. I do so because the risks presented by the pandemic required all court systems to contemplate ways to move at least some parts of their operations online. As courts across the country were obliged to consider the ways to maintain some degree of their workloads in a "stay at home" world, state supreme courts and state-level administrators in every state crafted policies that gave either limited or comprehensive attention to the incorporation of technology into the work of their courts. Given the universality of the pandemic's threat to public health, and the requirement to design remote ways of work as a consequence, we thus can compare approaches to a similar policy challenge across state systems.

Selecting States for Analysis: High Courts with
Greater and Lesser Control over Technology-Related
Administrative Authorities

In order to study how a state high court's level of administrative authority affects its communication of preferences over case processing and court operations, I focus on a specific policy dilemma: the transition to virtual and hybrid (combinations of remote and in-person participation) activities in courts. To effectively modify and support the use of technological tools, courts must have the resources and authority to enforce compliance with their decisions. Therefore, if the power to obtain and manage technologies and court facilities is controlled by central actors, they will be responsible for making decisions about the technologies their systems adopt and will have a significant impact on the processes that determine the implementation of these choices.[5] In comparison, if lower courts have control over these administrative tools, state supreme courts and state level administrators will likely have less of an influence on lower courts' adoption and use of specific technologies.

To understand how central actors in court systems can influence the use of technology and other resources in transitioning to a remote work environment, I used data from the 2016 State Court Organization (SCO) survey administered by the National Center for State Courts (NCSC). This survey asked state court administrators about their control over various aspects of court administration, including those that are relevant to the adoption and management of technological tools: records management, emergency management, facilities management, facilities security, budget preparation, purchasing, human resources, and information technology. I used this dataset to create a measure of centralization based on the reported level of control central actors had over these administrative powers.[6] By examining the relationship between this specific group of powers and state supreme courts' policy responses to the pandemic, we can better understand how central actors' ability to direct the work of those within their court systems is impacted by different policy situations.

The scaled variable reveals that states do vary quite a bit in their assignment of these administrative powers, with states representing nearly the entire range of possible scores (range = 9–24, mean = 16.4, SD = 3.7). In most states, these management responsibilities were most commonly shared between lower courts and statewide offices. However, it was not unusual for statewide offices to control budget preparation and information technology, and for local authorities to manage facilities governance. The states, according to their centralization rating on this scale, are organized in table 2.1 and presented visually using spider plots in figure 2.1.

The most decentralized states, or those states with scores placing them in the bottom 25 percent of the distribution, had administrators report that they did not have total control over any of the included policy areas. They did vary in the number of powers they shared, from Nevada and Texas only sharing information technology responsibilities, to Tennessee, where state court administrators reported that local courts only controlled records management, with all other authorities shared. Washington is an outlier in the group, as it is the only state in the bottom quartile with one centralized power (emergency management), locally controlling or sharing control over all areas.

States scoring in the top 25 percent, or the most centralized states on this measure, had administrators report that no powers were unilaterally controlled by local court actors. States in this category reported total control over all relevant categories (Rhode Island, Vermont, Connecticut), over a majority of the categories (West Virginia, Massachusetts, Alabama), exerted

Table 2.1. States by Remote-Relevant Administrative Centralization Score Quartile

Lower 25%	50th Percentile	Upper 25%
Florida,[a] Indiana, **Louisiana**, **Michigan**, **Missouri**, **Nevada**, **Ohio**, Pennsylvania, South Carolina, **Texas**, Washington[b]	Alaska, **Arizona**, California, Delaware, Georgia, Illinois, Iowa, Kansas, Maryland, **Minnesota**, Mississippi, New Jersey, **New Mexico**, North Carolina, North Dakota, **Oregon**, **Tennessee**,[c] Utah, **Wisconsin**	**Alabama**, **Arkansas**, Colorado, **Connecticut**, **Hawai`i**, **Kentucky**, **Massachusetts**, New Hampshire, South Dakota, **Rhode Island**, **Vermont**, West Virginia

[a] Bold indicates a state that is included in the document analysis described below. States that did not submit responses to the NCSC SCO survey include ID, ME, MT, NE, NY, OK, VA, and WY.

[b] While scoring within the 25th percentile, Washington is the only state in this group with an authority that was centrally controlled.

[c] While scoring above the 25th percentile, Tennessee is the only state in the middle 50% that has at least one locally controlled administrative authority and no centrally controlled authorities.

total control over half and shared control over the other (Arkansas, Hawai`i), or reported 3/8 of the authorities as centrally controlled (Colorado, Kentucky, New Hampshire). States in the middle 50 percent of the distribution either reported different combinations of total, local, and shared control (California, Kansas, Mississippi, North Carolina), shared all powers (Arizona, Delaware, Maryland, New Jersey, New Mexico, Oregon, South Dakota) or shared control of six or seven of the eight authorities (Illinois, Utah, Wisconsin, Alaska, Iowa).

Sampling principally from the states representing the top and bottom 25 percent of the centralization score distribution, the following analysis considers all collected policy documents that were distributed by state supreme courts and central administrators between March 1, 2020, and July 1, 2020. This initial four-month period was selected as it represents a time of high policy activity, covering a span of time when state supreme courts were promulgating orders at the highest frequency across the first year of the pandemic. This period also allows us to observe how states' policy responses evolved as the scope of the pandemic's threat came to be more clearly understood.

During this time period, the selected states collectively promulgated over 750 new and amended policy documents on their court systems' websites. I collected and archived these documents with the assistance of a team of research assistants on a rolling basis throughout the study period. Subsequently, I reviewed the documents using a multi-stage thematic analysis strategy. This strategy was informed by the key research questions in this chapter, as well as by the approaches other scholars have taken to typologizing or otherwise distinguishing between features of policy instruments as mentioned earlier in the chapter (see also Bingham and Witkowsky 2021).

In the first stage of the analysis process, I familiarized myself with the content of the documents in my sample (see generally Ritchie and Spencer 2002). The goals of this stage were simple: I wanted to understand the scope of the content of these documents, the intended audiences for them (e.g., court administrators, judges, courthouse employees, employees of other governmental agencies), and the approaches state high courts used to present information to these audiences. In other words, in addition to immersing myself in the text, I wanted to comprehensively assess if this document corpus was an appropriate data source to study the research questions at hand.

While the preliminary stage of the analysis confirmed the appropriateness of the data, it also revealed that not all documents distributed by state high courts during this time period were pertinent to the study. Therefore, in a second stage of review, I reread the documents and excluded those from the corpus that did not contain language pertaining to a state supreme court's approach to adopting remote technologies for civil case processing. Eliminated documents included those with a single substantive focus unconnected to the transition to the remote environment and those exclusively addressing policy changes related to criminal legal processes (e.g., a document containing a single provision solely focused on the use of videoconferencing in bail hearings). In total, about a third of the documents contained information judged to be relevant to how a state supreme court would approach the transition to a remote or otherwise modified civil docket.

In the third stage of the review, I conducted a close read of the remaining documents with the aim of annotating all instances of language that high courts used to communicate information about transitioning to the remote environment within the remaining documents. Subsequently, I classified these units of text according to the features of the policy instruments they conveyed using a thematic analysis. The initial categorization drew upon insights from the literature review; however, I remained open to the possibility of identifying additional, distinct features of supreme courts' policy messages (Liu and Van de Walle 2020, 739). Said another way, although the corpus contained features of policy instruments that sought to limit deviations from a high court's preferred course of action (e.g., restrictions on acceptable technology infrastructure), as well as those that conveyed more leniency and permission of discretionary behavior on the part of lower courts (e.g., the modification or suspension of barriers to modifying procedure at the local level), understanding how these features specifically manifested in the context of judicial procedure-making necessitated being open to varied presentations in the data.

Table 2.2 provides a snapshot of the results of the language classification method employed to organize the themes discussed in the results section below. It demonstrates the method using policy language conveying information about specific procedural steps (case processing and determinations of hearing modality) and local procedure-making processes themselves. The table is presented with a cautionary note, as I wish to emphasize the limitations of selecting text excerpts to display in this format. This method of data presentation may obscure nuances best explored through the consideration of the document's full text and the range of additional provisions therein.

Nevertheless, this table is instructive on a couple of dimensions. First, the table reveals an intermediate category of language used by state supreme courts. This category is neither entirely restrictive nor wholly permissive or delegatory. In my review of the documents, I found that some state supreme courts offered lower courts flexibility to make choices that reflected their local contexts, but only in specific substantive areas or for certain procedural actions, necessitating the creation of a flexible, intermediate category of policy language choice. Within the categories outlined in the table, the example texts offer relatively clear instances of supreme court policy language. These selections illustrate how supreme courts granted lower courts broad authority to enact local procedural changes, extended grants in specific areas, or imposed substantial constraints, sometimes offering no discretion to lower courts.

The Impact of Administrative Capacity on State Supreme Courts' Approaches to Constructing Remote and Hybrid Processes

In the early orders promulgated in the most centralized states according to the measure, state supreme courts were more likely to direct their systems' transitions to remote work, often by maintaining control over technological tools and other resources. In contrast, decentralized courts' supreme courts were more likely to offer suggestions and encouragement for utilizing technology and tended to support these efforts by delegating authority to lower court administrators and presiding judges and by offering incentives to implement their desired policy changes. Both centralized and decentralized states sought advice from those working outside of statewide offices. However, centralized states tended to exercise more monitoring authority, with decentralized states employing it in a more limited set of circumstances later in the period analyzed. These findings are generally consistent with the relationship as articulated above—central actors in highly centralized court systems had more tools at their disposal to enforce uniformity and exercised that authority accordingly during this period. The analysis also reveals how considering different elements of the scale in isolation may help us better understand

Table 2.2. Example Order Language by Level of Authority Extended to Lower Courts

Definition	Example Areas		
	Case Filing	**Hearings**	**Rules Changes Processes**
	BROAD LOCAL AUTHORITY		
Lower courts have broad authority; any existing barriers* to local-level procedural change removed; supreme courts and state-level administrators offer suggestions and guidance on how to approach change	"Judges presiding over a civil case . . . may exercise their discretion to waive . . . any filing deadlines or time limitations set through Missouri's e-filing system or by court order, local rule, or MO SCt. Rules 41 through 81." *Missouri S.Ct. 3/22/20* "Not all provisions . . . will be appropriate in each District. However, the form provisions are offered to assist the District Courts in	"In civil cases, trial courts should maximize the use of technology to enable and/or require parties to participate remotely." *Michigan S.Ct. 3/15/20* "Any requirement in a rule of the Court that a party appear in person or requiring in-person service may be waived by the Court, local court, hearing panel, board, or commission, as applicable." *Ohio S.Ct. 5/15/20* "All matters should continue	"For purposes of implementing procedural matters during this time, the provisions of Rule 18(C) of the Rules of the Tennessee Supreme Court are suspended to allow judges to issue general orders." *Tennessee S.Ct. 5/26/20*

to be conducted with the use of video and telephone conferencing whenever possible."

Louisiana S.Ct. 5/15/20

reviewing and updating the administrative orders."

Nevada S.Ct. 4/10/20

"Although our courts rely heavily on fines, costs, and fees to operate the court system, out of concern for the safety and welfare of Louisiana citizens I ask you to consider the following actions regarding those fines, fees, and costs."

Louisiana S.Ct. 4/21/20

LIMITED LOCAL AUTHORITY

Lower courts granted a specific scope of authority over stages or parts of civil case processing; supreme courts offer a restricted set of choices/options that are permissible

"During the state of emergency . . . the following rules are temporarily amended. . . . All service of process under this rule must be performed using electronic means (e-Filing

"Notwithstanding the suspension of nonemergency hearings in paragraph 3, in their discretion, Superior Judges may conduct nonevidentiary hearings in nonemergency matters

"Each chief . . . judge is encouraged to . . . enter local court rules regarding any . . . changes in local procedure, consistent with this Order. Notwithstanding the requirement . . . that proposed local rules be published and

(continued on the next page)

Table 2.2. *Continued*

	Example Areas		
Definition	**Case Filing**	**Hearings**	**Rules Changes Processes**
	where available, email, or fax, where available) to the greatest extent possible." *Michigan S.Ct. 4/17/20*	if all participants participate remotely." *Vermont S.Ct. 3/18/20* "Regarding family matters, we have identified two areas that may be addressed remotely." *Connecticut Chief Admin. 4/14/20*	submitted to the local bar and circuit court clerk(s), any proposed local court orders or rules shall have binding effect if submitted with majority support of the judges and approved by the Chief Justice." *Kentucky S.Ct. 5/15/20*

CENTRALIZED CONTROL

Supreme courts control all policy changes; no choices offered to lower courts	"In Superior Court divisions and units where there is no electronic filing rule that requires a specified means of service . . . service of pleadings and other papers (other than process) must be made by *Alabama AOC 4/8/20*	"The Unified Judicial System (UJS) went live with virtual court hearings. . . . Bottom line is that we feel confident using Zoom Professional software in the UJS."	Wisconsin Stat. § 751.12 sets forth procedures that the [Supreme C]ourt has employed for promulgating rules . . . in all courts. . . . The serious public safety risks associated with conducting a public hearing during the COVID-19

the following means."
Vermont S.Ct. 3/16/20

"The family court of each circuit shall provide an email address for such filings.... The family court in each circuit shall establish the procedures necessary to implement this order in their respective courts."
Hawai'i S.Ct. 4/9/20

"Judges must use available telephonic and video technology to conduct all hearings, unless the parties are unable to participate remotely."
Kentucky S.Ct. 3/26/20

pandemic require the court to act at this time. The public hearing on the Interim Rule is duly noticed in accordance with the deadlines set forth in Wis. Stat. § 751.12 (requiring notice not more than 60 days nor less than 30 days before the date of hearing)."
Wisconsin S.Ct. 3/31/20

"Suspension of existing rules and the adoption of the new rule shall remain in effect for the duration of the declared emergency or until such time, as soon as practicable, as a meeting of the Superior Court Judges can be convened to consider a vote on the changes."
Connecticut Superior Court Rules Cmte. (statewide) 3/20/20

* All barriers barring those that conflict with constitutional or statutory rights/rules/protections.

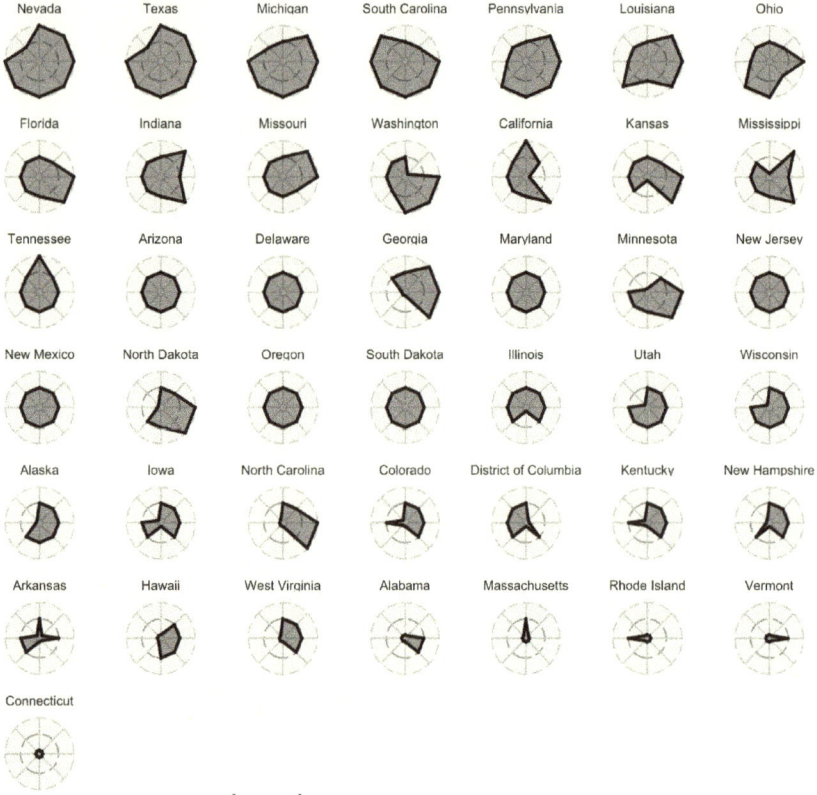

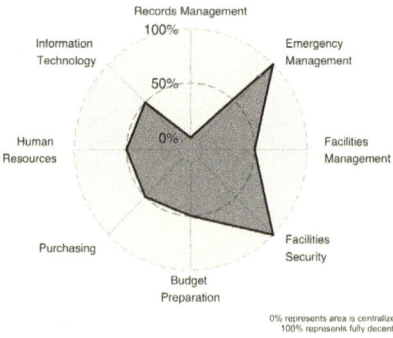

Figure 2.1. Differences in the level of remote-relevant administrative centralization by state

Source: NCSC Court Statistics Project, State Court Organization survey (2016), data archived by Weinstein-Tull (2020).

the top-heavier or more locally controlled methods employed by state supreme courts in systems in the middle 50 percent of the scale. The following subsections are organized thematically and describe general trends identified in the data.

Control over the Tools and Resources Necessary to Transition to the Remote Environment

The review of policy documents showed that the state supreme courts in systems with the highest centralization scores were more likely to direct their systems' transition to remote work, both in terms of their management of court employees and the services their courts provided to the public. These supreme courts typically did so by asserting control over technological tools and other resources. They also tended to maintain control over the processes that allowed lower courts to change their own local rules and guidelines in response to the pandemic.

In some highly centralized states, controlling the direction of the transition to the remote environment involved supreme court and statewide administrators' assertion of control over the types of technologies courts in their systems were to use. In some cases, this meant the selection of a particular software or technology's use. For example, in early April 2020, Alabama's statewide administrator sent a memo to members of the Alabama State Bar regarding the branch's decision to use Zoom Professional for all judicial business requiring videoconferencing.[7] The memo's purpose was to address concerns that Alabama lawyers were relaying about the security of Zoom. The administrator addressed these concerns and noted that he felt "confident using Zoom Professional software in the [Unified Judicial System]."

Centralized court systems often provided support and training to ensure that the technologies they chose were being used in the way they intended. Developing supportive infrastructure was likely necessary to ensure proper usage of these tools by lower courts. In the aforementioned Alabama memo, the administrative director also referenced trainings managed by the statewide IT division and explained how these trainings incorporated modules on ensuring the security of a Zoom meeting. Alabama was not alone among the centralized states in referencing state-managed technology trainings. For example, in a May 15 memo to judges and other judicial branch employees, the chief justice of Kentucky referenced the statewide administrative office's series of regional trainings on safety measures,[8] and in a June 5 memo the chief justice announced that, because all "circuit, family, and district court judges and staff now have access to online tools that let them prepare and submit orders electronically," online training materials had been developed by the administrative office, and individual courts could also request a training session with a member of the office's staff.[9]

Training related to the use of a mandated, statewide tool or course of action was very different from the approach taken in the more decentralized states. In these states, it was common for state supreme courts, administrative offices, and the ad hoc committees these institutions established to develop trainings and resources to support their preferred approaches to the adoption of technology and remote practices—but these materials were not usually accompanied by mandatory adoption language because these actors lacked an ability to force a particular course of action. For example, across multiple orders and announcements, Michigan's Supreme Court promoted resources to assist lower courts, including (1) decision charts regarding the making of choices about which cases should proceed remotely or needed to be held in person, (2) guidance on how to complete forms electronically, (3) multiple "frequently asked questions" documents pertaining to the use of remote technology, (4) guidance on how to use mail forwarding services, and (5) guidance on how to engage self-represented litigants in particular in the remote environment.[10] While Michigan's statewide actors were prolific distributors of this form of remote support, other states like Ohio, Texas, and Missouri provided resources to help their courts maximize remote participation, incorporate additional "non-essential hearings" into remote caseloads, and provided ideas for how courts with specialized dockets could transition to remote.[11]

There were also differences in how the more centralized and more decentralized states approached the advancement of alternatives. States with more decentralized court systems tended to provide options and suggestions for how lower courts could transition to remote operations, rather than mandating a specific approach. This more flexible approach permitted experimentation at the local level, but also indicated the preferred options of the state supreme court offering the suggestions. Michigan offers a compelling example of this method. In the Michigan Supreme Court's March 18, 2020, order, it recognized the potential for courthouse closures, urging courts to collaborate with county clerks to "ensure . . . court pleadings will continue to be accepted for filing by other means, such as U.S. mail, e-Filing, email, or facsimile."[12] Subsequent orders that mentioned electronic filing took steps to remove barriers to using e-filing methods across different document exchange contexts. For example, in the Court's April 17, 2020 order, it temporarily amended rules related to service of process (along with other rules changes). Here, the Court again acknowledged that e-filing was encouraged as a means of service "where available," and other electronic methods were also allowed as acceptable methods (e.g., e-mail). Although evidence—in these orders and in actions preceding the pandemic—would support the Michigan Supreme Court's preference for statewide e-filing, such a system did not exist.[13] As a consequence, the Court instead worked to create opportunities that encouraged the use of e-filing in its system's courts while advancing language supportive of a range of alternatives in parallel.[14]

State supreme courts in decentralized systems also suggested that lower courts recognize litigants' potential pandemic-related financial difficulties by waiving remote participation fees,[15] encouraged the use of alternative methods of filing documents—like physical drop-boxes and e-mail-based solutions[16]—and proposed creative methods of supporting self-represented litigants' technology needs, by, for example, making courthouse computer terminals publicly available to facilitate easier participation in videoconferencing and access to e-filing methods.[17] At their broadest, suggestions of alternatives took the form of requesting that lower courts make "all reasonable" and "good faith" efforts to utilize available technological tools.[18]

In more centralized states, alternatives were presented as necessary additions to existing sets of court procedures. The difference between the language used by decentralized and centralized systems becomes evident when comparing language detailing requirements for offering parties alternative methods of filing documents. In Tennessee, which has a more decentralized court system, courts were "urged" to use "available technologies, including alternative means of filing"—language the supreme court employed across multiple orders.[19] However, language used in Massachusetts, Vermont, and Connecticut—three states with more centralized judiciaries—was more prescriptive. In Massachusetts, trial court departments were ordered to "provide departmental-wide guidance . . . as to how, in addition to by mail and, when available, electronic filing, pleadings and other documents can be filed without coming to [a courthouse]."[20] In Vermont, the Supreme Court directed jurisdictions that had implemented e-filing systems to continue using them and permitted all parties in other jurisdictions to file documents via e-mail.[21] In Connecticut, the Supreme Court took steps to make it easier for self-represented litigants statewide to access the state's e-filing system.[22]

Making Temporary Rules of General and Local Applicability

Another key area of difference concerned that of how state supreme courts managed the promulgation of orders and temporary rules changes by lower courts. Under normal circumstances, the promulgation of local court rules occurs through processes like those outlined in the previous chapter. During the pandemic, decentralized court systems removed obstacles that would normally prevent lower courts from quickly changing their rules and procedures. This allowed lower courts to have more freedom to use technology in their operations. For example, in a late May 2020 order, the Tennessee Supreme Court suspended, "for the purposes of procedural matters during this time, the provisions of Rule 18(c)"—the Supreme Court rule governing the methods of promulgating local orders—"to allow judges to issue general orders."[23] Similarly, in a very early order, the Florida Supreme Court encouraged lower courts to establish their own temporary procedures—later in the study period, the Court solicited proposals for changes from an ad hoc working group to the uniform rules given their experiences under modified rules during the pandemic.[24]

In contrast, some centralized states took the approach of slightly modifying local rule adoption procedures, whereas others maintained the status quo processes for doing so. For example, the Kentucky Supreme Court did remove some barriers to local rule promulgation by eliminating the requirement for lower courts to solicit feedback from their local bar associations and clerks in an early step of the adoption process, but it maintained the requirement that such rules had to be approved by a majority vote of the judges within the jurisdiction Court and receive approval by the chief justice.[25] The Connecticut Supreme Court convened a statewide committee to determine which rules affecting superior courts could be temporarily suspended or adopted, further articulating that permanent changes to any rules would be made through extant processes.[26]

Another way that the more centralized court systems' central actors maintained control over the transition to remote and hybrid actions was by retaining the authority to change the rules altogether. One way that they did this was through modifications or clarifications of preexisting Supreme Court rules and rules of practice. For example, the Hawai`i Supreme Court permitted remote appearances within the boundaries of extant law and procedure, and the Massachusetts Supreme Court clarified that electronic signatures were acceptable in the place of wet signatures under extant court rules.[27] While the more decentralized states also clarified uniform rules with respect to electronic seals,[28] the use of electronic signatures across a number of pleading types,[29] and approved alternative methods to serve summonses and to conduct alternative depositions,[30] it was much more common for them to remove the barriers to the implementation of technological solutions entirely[31] as compared to the centralized states.[32]

In conjunction with removing the barriers to lower courts' adoption of their own temporary orders and rules changes to respond to the pandemic, supreme courts in the more decentralized states were more likely to explicitly delegate authority to presiding judges and other people in administrative roles to make the call about the appropriateness of remote hearings and appearances.[33] While centralized courts also included provisions in their orders that delegated authority to people in these positions to make the determination about the appropriate use of technologies in their courts, these permissions tended to be granted later in the study period as compared to the decentralized systems.[34]

Approaches to Monitoring and Ensuring Compliance

As the most administratively centralized states' supreme courts directed the response in their states, they also crafted ways to monitor the actions of subordinate courts. In contrast, states with higher levels of local administrative control tended to exercise monitoring authority later in the study period and focused more on the approval of plans to transition back to in-person operations. In some of the states with highly centralized court systems, the state supreme court took an active role in monitoring the implementation of the plans it had crafted for transitioning to remote operations during the pandemic. For example, the Alabama Supreme Court permitted lower courts to have stricter restrictions regarding in-person appearances than the Court had promulgated, but required those courts to get approval from the Supreme Court before implementing them.[35] State supreme courts also required lower courts to submit local orders articulating how they would implement their supreme court's plan.[36] In Rhode Island, the Court required lower courts to submit plans for conducting nonessential hearings online, including details about how the public would access the hearings, for its approval.[37] These courts also articulated that the specific actions of lower courts, like their use of videoconferencing software, would be monitored by the statewide administrative office.[38]

In comparison, in states with more decentralized court systems, state supreme courts often took a more hands-off approach to monitoring the transition to remote operations. In these states, supreme courts typically intervened later in the study period as compared to the most centralized states, and they tended to request information from lower courts as it pertained to reopening or expanding operations.[39] An outlier among the more decentralized states in this regard was Indiana: throughout the study period, the Supreme Court strictly adhered to its rules regarding emergency relief: lower courts were required to petition the Supreme Court for permission to adopt locally applicable orders responsive to the pandemic.[40] Supreme courts in decentralized states also monitored lower courts by assigning authority to regional presiding judges to monitor and ensure compliance with guidance promulgated by the Supreme Court and statewide administrative office.[41]

Common Features across System Types: Acknowledging Concurrent Authorities and Advice-Seeking Behavior

State supreme courts in both centralized and decentralized systems acknowledged the ways in which concurrent authorities (e.g., gubernatorial orders, statutes) limited their ability to act with respect to some areas of case processing. A prominent example was that of the rules pertaining to signing and establishing the authenticity of certain documents. Before the pandemic, many jurisdictions permitted lawyers to submit documents accompanied by an assertion of their veracity under penalty of perjury but required self-represented litigants to submit documents signed in the presence of a notary public for an equivalent legal effect. While some courts had adopted the method of remote online notarization (RON) (or had done away with a notarization requirement for court documents entirely) or accepted e-signatures for certain types of documents filed electronically, some state supreme courts were limited in their ability to implement changes to notarization policies because in those states, notarization was a statutory matter that the court system could not unilaterally amend.[42]

These statutes were on the books in states with both centralized and decentralized court systems, and state supreme courts acknowledged their inability to modify these provisions.[43] For example, the Rhode Island Supreme Court acknowledged in an early April 2020 order that it was able to apply an interpretation of a Supreme Court rule to accommodate e-signatures for electronic filing purposes, while notarization was a matter out of its hands.[44] In Vermont, another state with a more centralized court system, the Supreme Court reported that it had asked the legislature for a temporary relaxation of notarization standards and alerted courts that the accommodation was approved, allowing parties to file documents under a temporary perjury standard.[45] And while supreme courts in the most decentralized systems also acknowledged statutory control of notarization,[46] they also took steps to work around these requirements. For example, in Ohio, the Supreme Court reported that it had conducted a review of court forms, temporarily revising them to not require a notary when applicable.[47]

State supreme courts in centralized and decentralized systems also established workgroups, ad hoc committees, and task forces to facilitate their approach to pandemic response. These groups were charged with a number of responsibilities, including making recommendations about essential court functions,[48] devising plans for the return to full operations,[49] and facilitating the continuity of court operations.[50] These groups produced a number of work products as a consequence, including model orders for lower courts,[51] bench cards, best practices guides, and other types of online resources and tools.[52] In forming these groups, state supreme courts in both centralized and decentralized systems likely perceived value in gaining information about local conditions from those working in positions both within and outside of the state's judiciary. In addition to the informational benefits, the solicitation of input from those outside of statewide offices may have served to foster a sense of legitimacy of the choices made by central actors—a topic that will be addressed in more detail in the following chapter. Supreme courts in both types of systems also encouraged lower courts to liaise with local officials, including clerks and local health departments.[53]

Explaining (Seemingly) Counterintuitive Findings

The document review revealed that state supreme courts with more centralized control over the administration of their court systems tended to take a different approach to directing their systems' transition to remote work than those with less control. However, the review also revealed that simply looking at a global measure of centralization may not be sufficiently nuanced to explain a state supreme court's actions. In addition to detecting trends among members of the most and least centralized groups given an additive measure of administrative control, it is important to consider a supreme court's level of authority in specific areas of authority in order to better understand its behavior. For example, in Arkansas, where the court system received a high score on the additive measure of the centralization of technological tools, the Supreme Court urged lower court officials to cooperate and establish relationships with county officials.[54] If the measure is deconstructed, this local-level cooperation may be a function of the fact that the Arkansas courts share responsibility over the management of buildings where their courts are sited. In the same early March 2020 memo, the chief justice of the Arkansas Supreme Court also acknowledged that courts could use court-automation funds to support the purchase of Zoom licenses or other software. This would suggest more local control given that it was phrased more as advice—lower courts could take a course of action if they wished. Such a statement would seem puzzling by looking at the global measure, but state court administrators responding to the NCSC survey reported sharing control over purchasing with lower courts. While the scale approach is useful for gauging the degree of administrative centralization in a court system, examining specific components may enhance our understanding of why state supreme courts may have produced seemingly counterintuitive policy language.

By scrutinizing and deconstructing the centralization score, we can also gain insight into why states that scored in the middle of the scale may have exhibited behaviors similar to those states that were the most administratively centralized or decentralized according to the scale. For instance, court administrators in Utah and Iowa reported in the NCSC survey that statewide actors had complete control over information technology (in Utah's case) and budget preparation and information technology (in Iowa's case), while other remote-related responsibilities were shared with lower courts. In both states, supreme courts exhibited behavior that aligned with expectations of the actions of a high court in a highly centralized system.

In Utah, early orders from the Supreme Court emphasized the importance of a uniform response to the pandemic. For example, in an order dated March 13, 2020, the Court noted that due to a proliferation of orders across jurisdictions within the court system, "it [became] necessary to issue a single order to govern all courts," adding that its general order would "supersede all orders relating to the pandemic issued by any court or any district."[55] In addition to this order's now universally applicable provisions, like the requirement that alternative filing methods be made available to those parties who lacked access to e-filing, the Court retained control over how procedural changes would be made going forward. For example, like high courts in the more centralized states, the Utah Supreme Court tended to permit procedural modifications within the boundaries of extant law and process (e.g., permitting remote oaths). Not unlike both types of court systems described previously, the Utah Supreme Court also established a workgroup to assist the Court in directing the pandemic response. In a May 11 order, the Court acknowledged that the workgroup would be tasked with formulating a response plan for "the entire judiciary."[56] Given the workgroup's recommendations, the Supreme Court only permitted lower courts to increase their operations if they received the approval of the statewide administrative office.[57] During this time, the state limited local control by giving lower courts very little discretion in their operational choices.

Iowa tells a similar story. Iowa's statewide administrators

reported having total control over budget preparation and information technology, and early orders indicated that the state sought to maintain control over these functions. For example, an FAQ document on March 12, 2020, stated that the centralized information technology office alone would have the authority to design policies permitting court employees to take their work computers home.[58] In addition to asserting control over how physical technologies would be used in the state court system, Iowa took other actions to centralize the transition to the remote environment. In the states with more administrative decentralization, supreme courts commonly allowed lower courts to take necessary actions to respond to the pandemic by suspending all procedural and rule-based barriers that hindered the adoption of responsive procedures. However, Iowa's Supreme Court took a more specific approach by suspending barriers in a more explicit manner, specifying which barriers per order it was willing to remove for lower courts to act. The Court also maintained control by amending its own rules to allow for electronic signatures across the civil docket. But, while the more centralized states acknowledged how concurrent authorities constrained them (e.g., in the case of notarization requirements), Iowa took Ohio's approach and reviewed forms requiring notarization, revising them to permit a temporary perjury standard.[59]

Based on this review of documents disseminated by these states during the first four months of the pandemic, I have found evidence supportive of my central argument: the most centralized court systems tended to use policy language that permitted them to maintain control over the transition to remote work, while the supreme courts in more decentralized systems tended to use language that granted more autonomy to lower courts. Centralized systems mandated the use of specific technology tools and maintained strict control over lower court policies, whereas decentralized systems removed obstacles that hindered lower courts from making changes. While the global centralization scale applied in this chapter had its limitations, it provided a valuable framework for comparing the actions of state supreme courts operating in distinct institutional contexts.

Additionally, I found that examining specific components of the scale provided insights into why some courts behaved differently than expected based solely on their aggregate level of administrative centralization.

Understanding the Link between Administrative Power and High Courts' Pandemic-Era Policy Choices

This chapter began by asking how a state supreme court's level of practical administrative power is related to the methods by which it expresses its preferences on case processing and court operations policies. Since high courts may not have the same level of administrative power as they do in the adjudicatory sphere, I looked to literature outside of the judicial politics space to better understand how policymakers approach their role in creating policies when they vary in their level of control over the entities they regulate. The literatures on administrative law and public bureaucracy provided me with the necessary language to proceed with this analysis, as it presented the notion that policymakers have varying tools at their disposal depending on their ability to ensure compliance. The ability of administrators to require a particular type of activity is dependent on their power to monitor, compel, or incentivize behavior. In contrast, administrators in high-ranking positions across all types of organizations can benefit from sharing guidance and best practices. Such practices can cultivate feelings of legitimacy and trust among implementing groups, even for strong administrators, and serve as a means of conveying preferences for weaker administrators.

To explore these dynamics, I leveraged a survey conducted by the National Center for State Courts in 2016 wherein state-level court administrators were asked to report the level of control they exerted over different areas of practical authority, including over the use of technology, human resources, budgets, and building management. Most state supreme courts and central administrators do not possess complete control over all administrative powers that govern case processing and court operations in their states. Using an additive scale of measures most relevant to the transition to remote operations, I analyzed more than 750 documents promulgated by twenty-five different court systems, principally focusing on those with the highest and lowest centralization scores in this study. I analyzed the ways in which state supreme courts communicated their expectations for lower courts to adapt to remote operations during the pandemic, including any changes made to rules or procedures to facilitate this transition, any directives or mandates issued to lower courts, and any other actions taken by supreme courts to guide the implementation of their systems' response plans (e.g., establishing task forces, distributing guidance materials).

The findings of this document review exercise strengthen the empirical case for the argument advanced in this chapter. The most administratively centralized court systems tended to use policy tools that allowed them to maintain control over the processes related to the transition to remote operations. In contrast, supreme courts in decentralized systems tended to allow lower courts to experiment with policy choices that were most applicable to their local environments. The most centralized supreme courts achieved their goal by mandating the use of specific technology tools and maintaining the status quo regarding lower court rule changes and order promulgation policies. In contrast, the least centralized supreme courts tended to remove barriers that would impede lower courts from taking decisive action. While the scale used for categorizing court systems had its limitations, and no state supreme court perfectly adhered to the behavior that would be expected given its place on the scale, examining the specific components of the scale proved to be useful in explaining unexpected actions taken by state supreme courts.

In addition to supporting the application administrative policy design theories to the court administration context, I suspect that the empirical framework employed here could be extended to other types of policy choices made by supreme courts in the administrative arena. In the empirical section of this chapter, I suggested that because there really isn't a great way to summarize the centralization of a court's administrative structure with a single quantitative measure, scholars could instead consider which features of court administration they view as important to a particular policy dilemma. Considering those elements in isolation may reduce the noise created by other features of court administration that may muddy the analytical waters. For example, the NCSC survey employed in this chapter reveals that judicial education is controlled by a statewide office in twenty-four states (of the forty-three respondent states) and is either shared (seventeen) or controlled locally (two) in the remaining states. Scholars interested in how judges implement, for example, accommodations for self-represented litigants in the courtroom may find it fruitful to compare the proliferation of training tools across these categories of states, or to compare within- and between-state variation in how judges perform that guidance (see also Carpenter et al. 2022b). As another example, in the 2016 SCO survey, state court administrators also reported their level of authority over court-annexed alternative dispute resolution: in only six states did they report having total control over ADR programs. What might be the consequences of more uniform applications of ADR programs as compared to those that are locally managed? I discuss research opportunities pertinent to this latter example in this book's final chapter.

In the next chapter, I examine how the level of centralization in a state's court system affects the implementation of the transition to a remote environment by those working in lower courts. Using elite interviews across three court systems, I explore how these actors perceived of—and executed—their policymaking roles during the COVID-19 pandemic. I will argue that the behavior of lower court actors in both centralized and decentralized systems is best explained using a blend of elements from the hierarchical and local-control models of decision-making in courts.

3 | The View from Below
Investigating the Behaviors of Lower Court Actors in Response to Supreme Court Pandemic Policies

In the previous chapter I argued that the degree of centralized control of a court system's administrative policy tools would influence a supreme court's performance of its administrative authority. To explore this relationship, I looked to the ways in which these high courts directed the operations of their branches during the first four months of the pandemic. I developed an approach to measuring administrative centralization that placed state court systems on a continuum according to the degree to which they centralized the control of the administrative tools I judged to be most related to the transition to the remote/hybrid environment. After examining documents from supreme courts in different quartiles of the administrative tool centralization scale, I found that highly centralized systems tended to use policy tools and language that allowed them to retain more control over their systems' shift to remote operations while more decentralized systems tended to give lower courts more freedom to experiment with procedural choices responsive to their local contexts.

In this chapter I explore how lower court actors responded to the policy choices advanced by their supreme courts during the pandemic. Although the extent of a supreme court's formal control over specific administrative policy tools plays a critical role in shaping lower court adherence to the policies it sets, I contend that we can also detect differences in implementation behavior within systems. Here, I investigate how lower court actors' alignment with their supreme courts' preferences over certain procedural changes, combined with their own views on the best administrative strategies for their local situations, affects their approach to policy implementation.

First, I demonstrate the constraints of the hierarchical and local control models when considered in isolation, and argue that an integrative model is best suited to the study of administrative choices by lower court actors working within state court systems. The hierarchical account suggests that the administrative structure of a court system determines who has the authority to effectuate administrative power, but is limited in its ability to explain why lower court actors would choose to deviate (or not) from the preferences of high courts. Conversely, the local control account suggests that a perception of administrative distance from central actors leads to local-level deviations from supreme court preferences, but this model is limited in its ability to account for why some lower court actors may feel compelled to comply with a high court's operational preferences (Weinstein-Tull 2020, 1032). This chapter offers evidence suggesting that lower court actors may weigh a supreme court's possession of tools to coerce or incentivize the adoption of its preferred policy against their own preferences regarding court administration and their assessments of how high court policies fit their local contexts. When these factors are in competition, lower court actors may behave in ways that are not reflective of the preferences of their supreme courts.

The chapter builds on the argument presented in the previous chapter and incorporates further insights from the public bureaucracy and administration literatures, applying the rationales for compliance and defection to examine the dynamics between supreme courts and lower courts in the administrative sphere. It analyzes the policymaking activities of lower courts during the COVID-19 pandemic, drawing on interviews conducted with lower court actors in states where supreme courts have varying levels of control over relevant administrative policy tools. This analysis strengthens the case for the utility of an integrated account of these decision-making models within the administrative context.

Limited Tools, Varying Compliance: Understanding Administrative Power Dynamics from the Perspective of Implementers

Unlike in the adjudicatory context, where lower courts make decisions that can be monitored and corrected through the appellate process, the administrative domain is characterized by a varied range of behavior-shaping mechanisms across judicial systems according to their administrative design. While lower court actors are charged with implementing administrative decisions by high courts, state supreme courts and their central administrative bodies vary in their capacity to effectively rein in deviant behaviors by these implementers. This means that in some systems, lower court actors may not perceive costs to straying from the preferences of high courts in their implementation processes. What motivates a lower court actor to adhere to or deviate from a high court's preferred administrative policies? Understanding this variation is critical to appreciate the dynamics of policy implementation in the judicial branch, particularly in the administrative domain.

The bureaucracy and public administration literatures offer insights into the motivations driving implementers' behavior, identifying factors that influence how these populations approach carrying out the policies created by central actors. These factors may include the level of bureaucratic control exerted by central actors on implementers, implementers' consideration of the alignment between central actors' preferences and local conditions in their jurisdictions, and the availability of local jurisdictional resources that enable them to act independently.

In a highly centralized organization, those in leadership positions have greater capacity to assert administrative control compared to those in an administratively decentralized organization. This is because managers in the former type of organization have access to a broader range of policy tools to communicate their preferences and ensure their implementation by subordinates (Xiao and Zhu 2022; see also DeHart-Davis 2007; Scott 1997; Bozeman and Scott 1996; March, Schulz, and Zhou 2000). Central actors may formulate policies that either allow for flexible implementation or require strict adherence to their preferences. However, in highly centralized organizations, subordinates are often constrained in their discretion when making choices over how to carry out a policy directive, standing in contrast to more decentralized organizations. As a consequence, scholars note a reduction in instances of noncompliant behavior when an organization exhibits features of centralization (e.g., Xiao and Zhu 2022; Fleming 2020).

When central actors wield significant control over administrative tools that can coerce or incentivize compliance, they can more effectively influence and guide the behavior of subordinates in accordance with their preferences. One method of exercising this control entails monitoring subordinates' behavior, but monitoring often comes with high costs for central actors (see generally McCubbins and Schwartz 1984). Therefore, judicious deployment of this tool and the development of supplementary methods are necessary for fostering compliant behavior.[1] As such, principals in both centralized and decentralized organizations also rely on other strategies to motivate compliant behavior among those in subordinate positions.

In some organizations, central actors might use the allocation of material resources as a means to promote compliance. When employing a resource-based approach, the willingness of subordinates to comply with central actors' preferences can vary based on their perceptions of dependency on these central actors for the resources necessary to fulfill their responsibilities (DiMaggio 1988; Ferner and Edwards 1995; Weingast 2009; see also Xiao and Zhu 2022). This suggests that encouraging compliant behavior among implementers in well-resourced jurisdictions may be more challenging (Ferner and Edwards 1995; Weingast 2009). Conversely, subordinates in under-resourced jurisdictions may be inclined to act in ways that please central actors if they believe that compliant behavior will result in the provision of necessary resources (Zhu and Zhao 2018).

Central actors can also employ collaborative policymaking methods to promote compliant behavior. For example, principals may engage implementers in the decision-making process by soliciting their input on operational and procedural policy changes. This collaborative approach may foster a sense of co-ownership of policy outputs among subordinates, ultimately enhancing the probability of compliance (for a review, see Wang, Hou, and Li 2022).

To ensure adherence to the rules and procedures they communicate, central actors can make use of a variety of different tools and approaches at their disposal. Nevertheless, in complex organizations such as court systems, frontline workers may be inclined to adapt these rules and processes to the unique dynamics of their local environments. These localized influences can serve as motivating factors for them to deviate from central actors' prescribed methods of implementing policy choices. These deviations do not have to be wholesale rejections of principals' preferences. Instead, such behavior by local actors may be best characterized as a "micro practice" involving the "negotiation, adaptation, or the prioritization of some tasks over others" stemming from alternative rationales that may conflict with the principal's desired outcomes (Mavrot and Hadorn 2021, 3; Gofen 2015; Lipsky 1980).

Local forms of innovation or noncompliance may thus be driven by differences in the objectives and preferences of central and local actors (e.g., Lee and Park 2023; Hedge and Scicchitano 1994). This difference in perspective between central and local actors can result in a rejection of central policies that do not align with local conditions (Grossback, Nicholson-Crotty, and Peterson 2004; Volden 2006) as local implementers strive to protect their jurisdictions from centrally imposed guidelines that they perceive to be misaligned with their local contexts (see, e.g., Tummers et al. 2015; Andersson and Ostrom 2008; Ostrom, Schroeder, and Wynne 1993). Local actors may also find it difficult to accurately implement central actors' preferences due to perceived or actual conflicts between the rules that guide their behavior (Jewell and Glaser 2006).

The implementation of administrative policies within complex organizations is a process shaped by a variety of factors. Individuals responsible for executing these policies often find themselves balancing pressures from policy promulgators and their local environments, which can conflict with one another.

In hierarchical organizations, central actors may possess a high level of formal control over the execution of administrative policies, but they still need to assess the costs and benefits of utilizing the tools available to ensure compliance. Local implementers, in comparison, may exhibit varied likelihoods of adhering to the preferences of central actors according to their local contexts, perceptions of differing goals, and level of reliance on centralized resources. Misalignment with central actors on these dimensions can result in what is referred to as "street-level divergence" (Gofen 2015; see also Lipsky 1980). To gain insight as to why lower court actors make specific administrative policy choices, we must examine how local implementers interpret the policies set by central actors and how their perceptions of those policies influence their subsequent administrative activities.

A Case for Synthesizing Hierarchical and Local Accounts of Administrative Decision-Making in State Court Systems

Existing research has shown that court actors adapt procedures and make operational choices to suit their local contexts (e.g., Leib 2015; Sudeall and Pasciuti 2021, 1365, 1379; Carpenter et al. 2022b; Carpenter et al. 2018; see also Bookman and Shanahan 2022, Bookman and Noll 2017), but the empirical approaches in these studies are limited in their ability to determine the relative influence of hierarchical and local factors in the decision-making processes of these actors.[2] While the localized account of judicial administration is supported by evidence and theory, it typically isn't assessed in a manner that fully considers the potential effects of hierarchical dynamics. Studies of jurisdictions within single states (e.g., Leib 2015) and comparative descriptive studies of courts' organizational structures (and not of the policies they produce, necessarily) (e.g., Weinstein-Tull 2020) are limited in their ability to consider variation in the top-down structural constraints that may be present in a given court system. As a consequence, we miss out on an opportunity to observe the interaction between centralized explanations guided by the structural features of courts and decentralized explanations guided by local context.

As demonstrated in chapter 2, American state court systems' administrative arms vary in how they are structured, and thus vary in the degree to which they assign administrative powers to central actors (Gallas 1976; Schauffler 2007; Saari 1976). The organizational features of state judiciaries determine which actors get to make choices about how courts function. Some state judiciaries are more centrally administered, with procedural power concentrated in the state's supreme court and its statewide administrative office. In states with centralized judicial administration, lower courts have very little *formal* autonomy to independently design policy that fits their unique contexts. In more decentralized states, lower courts have considerably more formal power as the relationship between central management and these courts adheres less to a traditional hierarchical structure. In these systems, direction from high courts and state administrative offices could be considered as "advice" more often than they would be interpreted as a dictate or required course of action.

The organizational structure of a court system offers valuable information regarding the individuals and entities vested with the authority to create administrative policies. However, structure provides only limited insights into the practical implementation of this authority (Leib 2015). Given the literature reviewed in the previous section, there are reasons to anticipate that this authority may be utilized in ways that both conform to and deviate from the preferences of central actors. First, individual courts are not centrally located within a state; instead, they are geographically dispersed across it. As a result, distinct courts cater to diverse communities characterized by specific jurisdictional needs (Weinstein-Tull 2020, 1032). Moreover, there might be differences in how administrative matters are handled within these courts because of the distinctive viewpoints and administrative principles held by court actors, such as judges and court administrators, who work within them. These variances have the potential to shape their inclinations toward the management of their respective courts.

While attentiveness to structural variation in courts' administrative systems is important, incorporating local context and local actors' administrative preferences likely provides valuable additional context for why we might observe differences in lower courts' administrative policy behaviors within a given state court system. In administratively decentralized states, where lower courts are granted more authority to act responsive to their local contexts, we may not observe deviations from the supreme court's preferences if the actors in the lower courts perceive their administrative approach to be compatible with high court guidance. In other words, if lower court actors agree with high court actors about how administrative matters should be handled, they will defer not because they are required to do so, but instead because they agree with those working at the top of the hierarchy with whom they are aligned. Conversely, in centralized states, where lower courts offered less room to make locally applicable administrative choices due to the constraints presented by the administrative hierarchy, incompatibility with high court directives may spur these courts to take action, even in the face of monitoring or sanction. In these courts, the pull of their local context may weigh more heavily than these possible threats from above. These sources of variation thwart our ability to apply either a wholly local or a wholly hierarchical explanation of the administrative policymaking behaviors of lower court actors consistently and exclusively across state systems.

The expected behavior of lower court actors, as presented in table 3.1, highlights the combined influence of local context and formal authority on their administrative policymaking strategies. In states where the judicial system is less administratively hierarchical, granting lower courts greater authority in the administrative space, policy activity that deviates from high court preferences will be limited if they perceive alignment with high court guidance. In such cases, lower court actors will defer not out of obligation or fear of sanction, but because they share a common perspective with those at the top of the administrative hierarchy. Conversely, in states where the judiciary is characterized by a stronger administrative hierarchy, where lower court actors face greater formal constraints on their administrative ac-

Table 3.1. Predicted Categories of Local-Level Implementation Behavior in Response to State-Level Administrative Policy Decisions

	Structural Indicators	
Individual/ Local Indicators	**Weaker Administrative Hierarchy (more decentralized)**	**Stronger Administrative Hierarchy (more centralized)**
Misaligned local context/ administrative philosophy	High formal permission to act, high perception of local authority	Low formal permission to act, high perception of local authority
Aligned local context/ administrative philosophy	High formal permission to act, low perception of local authority	Low formal permission to act, low perception of local authority

tivities, a disconnect between local context and high court directives could prompt lower court actors to diverge from high court preferences, even in the presence of monitoring or sanctions. In these situations, local pressures may weigh more heavily on court actors than possible threats from above.

In sum, the organizational features of state judiciaries and the relationships between lower court actors and their local institutional contexts may influence the degree to which these actors feel compelled to craft administrative policies that fit their circumstances. In administratively decentralized states, lower courts are granted more authority to act in response to their local contexts, while in more centralized states, lower courts have less formal power. But working under a decentralized administrative regime does not necessitate local deviations from high court policy, nor does being in a centralized system entirely determine adherence to it. In both types of administrative arrangements, the attitudes and beliefs of court personnel can influence their perception of how local court operations should be managed, potentially leading to conflicts with higher court preferences. Even in the case of centralized states, lower courts may take informal action in response to their local contexts, regardless of monitoring or sanction from higher courts, if they perceive a mismatch between a supreme court's dictates and the needs of their communities. By recognizing the importance of both hierarchical and local factors, we can gain a better understanding of the complex administrative policymaking behaviors of lower court actors within state court systems.

Exploring Lower Court Responses to Supreme Court Administrative Actions during the Pandemic through Interviews

Prior scholarship has described features of court systems that lead to greater centralization or diffusion of decisional authority, but there has been limited ability to comparatively evaluate these accounts. Although this existing body of scholarly work has provided valuable insights into how courts design paths to case resolution and how litigants experience them, it tells us much less about the factors that determine who is making choices about the shape of those paths. States, which have the authority to design court systems suitable to their needs, vary in how they distribute power—across judges and other court actors and across levels of the hierarchy.

In March 2020, court systems were faced with a set of conditions that required the vast majority of them to rethink the ways they conducted business: the bulk of court operations prepandemic required lawyers, parties, jurors, non-lawyer advocates, court staff, judges, and others in the court ecosystem to be physically present to file paperwork, appear at hearings, and gather legal information—among other activities (Pollack 2021). The common exogenous shock presented by the COVID-19 pandemic thus allows us the opportunity to examine who in state court systems had the ability to weigh in on decisions about case processing while holding the pressure courts were facing somewhat constant. In other words, the pandemic gives us a chance to take a snapshot of the distribution of administrative decisional authority in state courts when the same general policy questions had to be answered across systems. At any other time before the pandemic, such a study would have been difficult to conduct given the different priorities of and pressures on state judiciaries.

To investigate the perceptions and behaviors of court actors engaged in the development and implementation of local administrative policies, I utilize the insights from the hierarchical and local control models, as synthesized in the preceding section, to frame my inquiry. I employ a semi-structured interview methodology as the primary means of data collection in three states that represent a diverse set of administrative structures (see generally Seawright and Gerring 2008; Gerring and Cojocaru 2016). Ultimately, by combining these theoretical frameworks and employing this empirical method, this research provides a more nuanced look into how high courts' monitoring capabilities intersect with the views of lower court actors regarding their own localized forms of administrative practice.

The empirical study of the policy choices of those working in courts is principally focused on understanding the inputs and outputs of adjudicative decisions made in cases. As a result, it is common practice to rely on written opinions and records of judges' votes alongside quantifiable predictors of behavior. However, adopting an approach that relies on what can be quantified limits our ability to thoroughly explore the decisional dynamics central to the goals of this chapter (Linos and Carlson 2017; Carpenter et al. 2022b). This is not to say that scholars interested in such questions are confined to using qualitative approaches—rather, I aim to clarify the scope and limitations of this work. Given that the main goal of this analysis is to broaden our insight into processes where empirical knowledge is scarce, the initial step in establishing a set of expectations depends on interpreting information regarding actors' perceptions. This involves learning more about their roles in decision-making processes and their interpretation of local contexts in relation to state-level considerations (Hochschild 2009).

As compared to other methods of collecting information on people's attitudes and behaviors, such as surveying or through observation, interviewing provides for a high level of participant engagement, which allows the researcher to probe and extract additional relevant themes (Kvale and Brinkmann 2009). Interviewing is especially valuable if the researcher seeks to understand and compare the perspectives of people involved in "processes of interest" across roles and political contexts (Tansey 2007, 769; Leuffen 2006; Carpenter et al. 2022b). Semi-structured interviews are particularly useful for elite interviewing, as this method allows the interviewer more flexibility in data gathering (Aberbach and Rockman 2002). Finally, and perhaps most obviously, an interview method is employed because it is best suited to the research questions relevant to this project (e.g., Carpenter et al. 2022b).[3]

The following sections outline an empirical strategy that considers the key sources of variation in lower court administrative contexts. It also details the data collection and analysis processes used in the study.

Selecting Study States Given Variation in Structural and Perceptual Indicators

In this section, I explain the key criteria used to select the states used in this chapter's analysis. First, I discuss the importance of accounting for the key characteristics of the administrative policymaking structures within these states, building on the insights of chapters 1 and 2. Additionally, I take into consideration the political backdrop against which court actors operate, emphasizing the significance of both accounting for and attempting to minimize sources of variation in the political environments surrounding these court actors. The adoption of the following case selection approach enables a deeper understanding of how lower court actors navigate the balance between their jurisdictional decision-making practices and the administrative policies set by their respective high courts.

Variation in the centralization and independence of court systems' administrative functions are key indicators used to compare the perceptions of those working within the study states' court systems. As presented in table 3.2, States B and C exhibit a greater degree of decentralization in their assignment of administrative authorities relevant to the transition to a remote environment. A detailed description of those authorities appeared in chapter 2. In contrast, State A has a far more centralized structure on these administrative dimensions.[4] Another potentially relevant factor, which was introduced in chapter 1, concerns the degree of independence that a given state court system has in making generally applicable rules and processes governing court business. In States A and B, the legislature plays a greater role in this process whereas in State C the legislature has not traditionally played a major role (Clopton 2018, 10). The distribution of these features across states enables comparisons to be drawn based on the degree of discretion lower courts have to craft locally applicable operational decisions, as well as the level of freedom generally afforded to a court system to make such choices.

These structural features give rise to a set of expectations regarding the way court actors working within these systems should discuss the distribution of administrative policymaking authority in the interviews. Court actors in State A should report that administrative authority is highly consolidated, with little room for local-level deviation from the policies set by these central actors. Court actors in State A should also report that the judicial branch is further constrained by its lack of administrative independence vis-à-vis the legislature. Court actors in State B should be similarly attentive to external constraints presented by the legislature but will likely report that lower courts have a greater level of administrative autonomy due to a decentralized administrative structure. Finally, we should expect court actors in State C to perceive a relatively greater level of autonomy in setting procedural and operational rules given the lack of legislative involvement in the rulemaking process. We should also expect court actors in State C to report that policymaking authority is distributed across courts in their state given its decentralized structure.

To account for the perceptual dimension, the study states were also selected according to their relative similarity on other key political dimensions. First, and as also shown in table 3.2,

Table 3.2. Court Structure and Political Characteristics of Study States

	State A	State B	State C
Administrative Structure	More centralized	More decentralized	More decentralized
Legislature Involved in Setting Court Rules/ Procedure*	Yes	Yes	No
State-Level Political Context	Unified Democratic control	Unified Democratic control	Unified Democratic control

* Clopton (2018).

all three states were under unified Democratic control of their state-level political institutions in the first year of the pandemic. This feature was judged as important to hold relatively constant as it helps to account for the types of messaging state high courts may have engaged in.[5] In these states, high court actors were more likely to have been in alignment with the plans crafted by the political branches of their state, in terms of their understanding of the scope of the pandemic's impact and plans for response. They may also have explicitly coordinated with the political branches on a response. Such features of court response are more likely in states with unified political control, where cooperation between branches is more probable. This type of political environment may contribute to greater autonomy given to court actors, as they may be trusted by the political branches to act, or less autonomy if the political branches chose to centralize power and direct court business.

Beyond the administrative policy environment as defined by the actions of high courts and central political actors, the local political context may also shape court personnel's perception of their independence and decision-making authority in relation to high courts. These views can be influenced by the opinions and needs of the local community (Leib 2015). The work of local trial courts inherently possesses a political dimension as they allocate the costs and benefits of policy choices within their communities and contribute to the formulation and refinement of the rules that govern how these communities operate. As a consequence, it is inevitable that people "holding different perspectives and expressing divergent concerns [would be] . . . interested in the business of courts and [are] anxious to influence the way they do business" (Corso 1979, 428; see also Mays and Taggart 1985).

In this study, it thus becomes important to consider the local contextual factors that may also influence those working in lower courts to depart from the operational preferences of their high courts. To be mindful of these factors, I consider a state's level of ideological heterogeneity in making my determinations of states targeted for this analysis (Tausanovitch and Warshaw 2013). I acknowledge that this is not a perfect indicator of administrative preferences at the local level. However, I suspect that by selecting states with levels of ideological diversity that are typical within the group of those with consistent state-level administrative messaging, I will create opportunities for an examination of the differences in how lower court actors make procedural choices that are (mis)aligned with high court preferences. This approach facilitates a more nuanced analysis of the factors influencing lower courts' procedural preferences in diverse institutional contexts. Specifically, by comparing States A, B, and C based on their administrative centralization and independence, and considering the political context of court actors, we can more thoughtfully assess the relative level of autonomy and flexibility afforded to lower courts in creating locally relevant operational policies.

Data Collection and Analysis Procedures

Engaging in research that requires access to judicial system actors and their work presents a unique set of challenges. While judges and court staff are a highly visible group that may initially appear readily recruitable through systematic or even randomized processes, their membership in this group significantly heightens their caution when considering requests for access to the knowledge they hold (Noy 2008; see also Atkinson and Flint 2001). With respect to recruiting judges in particular, Richard Posner noted in his 2010 book *How Judges Think* that "most judges are cagey, even coy, in discussing what they do" (Posner 2010, 2). Therefore, the sample for this study was primarily recruited through a relationship-based strategy, as "cold calling" (or e-mailing) court actors was deemed early on to be an inefficient approach for connecting with prospective interviewees from this elite population (Goldstein 2002, 669).

Following the selection of my target jurisdictions through the process described above, I next gained access to court actors by leveraging preexisting personal and professional relationships, as well as those connections formed as a result of my work liaising with the American Bar Foundation's COVID-19 Task Force.[6] These initial connections played a critical role in establishing the legitimacy of my project and in bolstering my own credentials and trustworthiness as I reached out to potential interview subjects (see, e.g., Nir 2018; Aberbach and Rockman 2002, 674). The resulting interview sample as detailed in table 3.3 includes nearly sixty participants, consisting of supreme court justices, trial and intermediate appellate-level judges, state court administrators, trial court administrators, clerks, and caseflow managers across three states (A, B, and C).[7] The sample is principally drawn from lower courts, and responses from those working in lower courts form the basis of the analysis that is reported in the proceeding section.

My coding and analysis processes were then guided by the strategies and practices advanced by Braun and Clarke for conducting a reflexive thematic analysis (2006, 2013). The first stage of the process, in which I familiarized myself with the data, was conducted as a parallel process to interviewing/data collection. Immediately after conducting an interview, I wrote out a set of rough notes summarizing my initial impressions of the conversation, including synopses of the ideas and attitudes brought up by the participant that were relevant to my research questions. After conducting a set of interviews, I began to form

Table 3.3. Interviews Completed per State by Position

State	A	B	C	N
Clerks and Court Staff	6	2	6	14
State-Level Administrators	2	3	1	6
Trial Court Administrators	1	9	0	10
Judges (Appellate and Trial)	2	14	12	28
N	11	28	19	58

an initial list of codes. To do so, I uploaded text transcripts that I hand-generated from audio recordings from the interviews to MAXQDA, a qualitative analysis software program. Using the program's interface, I carefully read the transcripts and assigned codes to the chunks of text that I viewed as relevant to the research question. In consultation with other experts in this field, I considered how different readings of the data might lead to different interpretations of the codes. This process helped me to refine and add nuance to my initial list of codes.

I then considered the relationships between my codes in the first iteration of theme development (Braun and Clarke 2006, 84, 87). These choices were informed by the literature's conceptualization of the constraints hierarchies impose and the ways local context influences compliance behavior, but I was also open to uncovering new connections between concepts and the data that were consistent with existing explanations, as well as to relationships that may have been previously considered as contradictory to existing theory. I was also careful to consider the internal consistency and the distinctions between different themes (Patton 1990). Throughout the consolidation process (from codes to themes) I was also attentive to the role my own assumptions played in the initial creation and adjustment of themes (Gough and Madill 2012). In this stage, I acknowledged my role as an interpreter of the data—themes did not "emerge" from the data; I played an active role in constructing them given the background knowledge I gained in the preliminary stages of the project and my familiarity with the theoretical approaches that informed the project's design.

Responding to Context or Following Orders?
A Comparison of Lower Court Actors' Behaviors
in Centralized and Decentralized Systems

In chapter 2 I identified that supreme courts in states with more centralized administrative powers tended to use policy tools that helped them maintain control over the direction of the transition to the remote environment. The interviews conducted for this chapter reveal that actors working in a highly centralized court system do perceive value in centralized management of administrative choices, providing examples of how central actors monitor lower court behavior and enforce compliance when they detect deviations from their chosen policies. But critically, respondents identified instances of deviation that they attributed as occurring because of a mismatch between local conditions and high court directives. When the local context had a stronger influence on court actors, lower court actors recalled instances of attempts to work around the rules set by the central actors.

In the case of the more administratively decentralized states, lower court actors provided examples of the policy strategies used by their state supreme courts in light of their inability to compel lower court behavior. The interviews also revealed that actors working within these systems were cognizant of the differences in the politics of and resources available to different jurisdictions within their states. They discussed the need to have flexibility in creating locally applicable policies as a consequence. They also mentioned the absence of monitoring in their systems, which they saw as providing opportunities for additional flexibility to experiment at the local level. Conversely, when lower court actors agreed with their supreme court's proposed policy solutions, they provided examples of why centrally managed administrative policy is valuable to them. For example, they perceived a political utility to having a higher court actor as a scapegoat for locally unpopular policies. Actors in under-resourced jurisdictions also acknowledged that the incentives offered to adopt their supreme court's preferred policies were hard to pass up, even if they may have disagreed with the policy choices that justified allocating the resources.

The results are discussed thematically. Themes related to the structural or hierarchical account of administrative authority include (1) the political and practical utility of relying on centralized authority and (2) the role of incentivizing deferral to central authority through the provision of resources. Themes related to a more decentralized account of administrative authority include (3) the perception of a policy vacuum at the top of the hierarchy and (4) a perceived mismatch between high court directives and the local context. A final theme, (5) perceptions of monitoring, relates to respondents' exercise of authority given the level of monitoring they perceived their high courts were exercising. Given the nature of the sampling strategy, I approach the interpretation and presentation of the findings with a degree of caution. With that said, the findings of this chapter suggest that future studies of administrative decision-making in court systems should consider the interplay between a system's level of centralization and the local context of its actors. Examined independently, neither factor is sufficient to capture the behaviors observed by lower court actors across the varied administrative designs of the systems discussed in this chapter.

Themes Related to Perceptions of Limited/Constrained Administrative Policymaking Authority

Actors across States A, B, and C identified reasons why they chose to follow directives given by high court and central administrative actors. The two major themes that emerged are (1) the political and practical utility of relying on centralized authority, and (2) resource provision incentivized deferral to central authority.

THE PRACTICAL AND POLITICAL UTILITY OF RELYING ON CENTRALIZED AUTHORITY

A first theme concerns actors' perceptions of the usefulness of following high court actions, thus limiting their independent policymaking authority. This was unsurprisingly a more common sentiment in State A, with actors acknowledging the value of centralized policymaking for both their work and the uniformity of experience for court users. Multiple court staff and clerks in State A reported this sentiment in the following ways:

> Being centralized allows us more uniformity so that when self-[represented parties] that might file a case here and then go file a case in [other State A jurisdiction] and maybe one at [another State A jurisdiction], that the process they use should be the same.
>
> I think uniformity is kind of key. You know, having a centralized branch—basically one director of court operations who—when we meet with them you know—we get the same message that "this is what we need to do, and here's how you need to do it or here's what you need to do." [This] makes the best sense to me. You're receiving the same kind of directives that should apply statewide.
>
> I think it's better that [the administrative policies were] coming from one location, generally. I mean, for the pandemic—making sure that we were all on the same page—especially because no one knew what was going to happen [from day to day].

Respondents from State A consistently reflected on the value of uniform application of court rules and procedures, and most often did so in the service of court users. Another member of a local court staff in State A posed a hypothetical scenario where two friends were talking at a bar about their divorce proceedings, which were happening in different parts of the state. One friend offers advice to the other to go to the courthouse and pick up a particular form. "You know, I feel bad for these two friends who are both getting divorced at the same time, but they can both have access to the same form. So that's good." Such an attitude is more likely to be predicted by a hierarchical account of judicial decision-making. Court actors in states with a centralized administrative structure tended to see the value of procedural homogeneity for court users. This perspective thus helps to demonstrate the utility of top-down models of administrative policymaking in state courts.

In States B and C, relying on centralized authority was seen as beneficial for some respondents due to the political advantages of depending on an authoritative source for managing court affairs during the pandemic. This was particularly true when re-spondents were dealing with other actors in their jurisdictions who might have been misaligned with the guidance provided by the high court. As examples, three judges who agreed with guidance coming from centralized sources said the following responsive to this theme:

> I certainly appreciated the order from [the state supreme court] where they said everybody's got to wear a mask. That was very help-ful for me because I was in [a county in State B] where the sheriff said "I'm not doing it."
>
> I was grateful for anything that I could use to reinforce the decisions that I needed to make. [I could] simply say, "Well, I am following the guidance of the [state] Supreme Court," and no one is going to argue in any courtroom [about that]. If . . . [I say,] "The supreme court has given me this directive and I am following the guidance of the supreme court," no one can say a word to me that I'm not doing something properly.
>
> If [the state supreme court] would not have given us coverage to be reasonable about [continuances with respect to speedy trial provisions] . . . to have the backing of the supreme court when we say, "Sorry, defendants, get comfortable" was very helpful. [Things] would've gone super poorly if they would not have given us cover-age.

When a respondent shared the view that high court or admin-istrative guidance was valuable to them, they not only sought to implement that policy but doubled down by leaning on the higher authority in order to demonstrate the legitimacy of their own actions. One judge in State B noted in a moment of expected pushback from others in the courthouse: "Without [supreme court] guidance, you're going to get a lot more blow-back. But when they come to me, I say, 'listen—our supreme court has said we need to do this.' And there's not much they can say in response." In the absence of supreme court guidance, an actor in State C lamented that the reactions from her local government made it difficult for the court to apply social dis-tancing requirements, remarking that "political cover—I think that would've been helpful."

INCENTIVIZING DEFERRAL TO CENTRAL AUTHORITY
VIA THE PROVISION OF RESOURCES

The second theme concerns actors' reflections on the incentives central administrative authorities offered in order to ensure consistent application of pandemic-related operations policies. The resources were often related to the provision of information technology equipment. This theme was most prevalent in States B and C, as central administration in State A didn't necessarily have to provide incentives to encourage consistency in implementation of policy. Notably, acknowledgement of utilization of state-level grant programs was most often heard in jurisdictions where court actors tended to disagree with the actions taken by central actors. In spite of this, they recognized that following guidance related to remote technology would also afford them an opportunity to upgrade courtrooms and workspaces—upgrades they could not have undertaken otherwise due to scarce resources.[8] Some examples from the judges, court administrators, and staff that spoke on this theme include:

> Our [local funding sources] were pretty much tapped out on resources, so we were more looking towards the state for funding for technology and things, and the grants that they made available [for technology].
>
> It is true that [the state supreme court] did help all the rural counties [in my jurisdiction] really upgrade a lot of the courtrooms. . . . I'm fully electronic now. While I'm running Zoom obviously you need extra monitors and extra things to really help that be efficient, so they helped us with the technology upgrades.
>
> I would say I am very happy that the state has given grants and has given money for updating technology. [The state] has given us the opportunity to say, "What could we have?" and "What could our technology look like?" and even provid[ed] consultants to come in and say, "This is what you need or what you could use."

These three statements suggest that in addition to administratively aligned court actors seeking the legitimization afforded by central policy choices, even actors that may have disagreed with the high court or administrator's approach adopted their preferred operations policies in exchange for the provision of resources. Take, for example, the judge who provided the final quote in the above section. This judge in State B, who said it was her "strongly held view that human interaction is far superior to technology-driven action," acknowledged that "there are some people that may think that I'm not progressive, that I'm behind the times." As demonstrated above, this same judge welcomed state funding to upgrade court technology and also ended up sitting on a statewide steering committee to formulate rules about technology. This judge's statements and behaviors are suggestive of another source of deference to central actors in decentralized systems: when resources are scarce, even those court actors opposed to high court directives will adopt them when provided with the means to do so.

Themes Related to Perceptions of Formal and Informal Policymaking Authority

Actors across States A, B, and C also identified reasons why they chose to generate their own administrative policy. In State A, these actions were more informal in nature as actors lacked the formal authorization to create policy responsive to the pandemic. The two major themes that emerged are (3) a lack of policy guidance and (4) the mismatch between central policy guidance and local context required local innovation.

STEPPING INTO THE POLICY BREACH

This theme concerns actors' perceptions of a lack of guidance from central sources. This view was most common in States B and C, and actors in these states perceived that this circumstance required them to use their authority to craft policy that may or may not have been consistent with supreme court or central administrative goals. Here, the distribution of authority to many sources results from perceived necessity—if a policy didn't exist to guide behavior, the actor viewed it was incumbent upon them or others in their jurisdiction to make policy. Selected statements that reflected this sentiment include:

> They weren't acting quickly enough. [Or] broadly enough. . . . They were taking a very conservative approach in how they were going to provide us with advice.
>
> We [were] stymied by the pace of some solutions. But I would say that we [had] been working on our pandemic plan since . . . right after 9/11 . . . and things progressed rapidly [in the first two weeks of March 2020]. The supreme court—we were constantly asking, "Hey, should we be considering closing? Should we be considering requiring masks?" They were always like, "Well, that's your choice."
>
> We had made huge adjustments to equipping our courtrooms—long before the [state's] administrative office had decided that. And that was because our county's IT had told us, "If we don't place an order for the TVs, the video cameras, the Zoom licenses early—we might not get it." So we had all courtrooms equipped before June 1. And the administrative office was just beginning to move on allowing virtual hearings. We'd already decided that.

This theme highlights the impact of the assignment of administrative authority to local level actors in decentralized court systems. In states where central administrators or high courts possess little formal authority, there may be a tendency for them to refrain from intervening in matters related to those policy areas. In some cases, the interview respondents were interested in the high court's perspective on matters, as demonstrated in the second quote above. Another actor in this state (B) remarked that the high court was "coming from behind." Although local level authority is expected in decentralized judiciaries, during the pandemic these actors often reported that they wished the central administrator or high court would have intervened. A member of court staff in State C said, "I wish that during this time period, they had stepped in and said, 'We're the boss of you and here's what you're going to do.' Because nobody knew what to do."

MISMATCH BETWEEN CENTRAL GUIDANCE AND LOCAL CONTEXT

The second theme concerned actors' perceptions of the fit of guidance from supreme courts and state administrators to their local context. In States B and C, policy mismatches were often ascribed to central actors' lack of appreciation of the diversity of circumstances within the state. If central guidance was perceived to be misaligned with the actor's goals, actors in these states were further motivated to ignore this guidance and generate novel operations policies. This dynamic is expected in decentralized states; local context weighs heavily on actors' behavior. Some examples from the judges, court administrators, and staff in States B and C who spoke on this theme include:

> It's potentially politically useful, right, to do things differently. And you know, I'm not saying I really don't believe what I'm saying or doing [in my position], I'm just saying that there's no consequence for doing what I want to do. It could be the other way around—you know—doing more than what's required. You know, making limitations on going to the courthouse more strict than is required.

> There has been in our [jurisdiction] a continuing feeling that [decisions about remote vs. in person] should be case by case, you know, or docket by docket. County by county. Because . . . we all have very different needs . . . in the different counties. We would like to think we know our population and litigants well enough to understand those needs.

> The [administrative office's] ideas are all well and good, but we need to think really carefully about how they apply given our knowledge of how people use our courts and the way that our local courts work.

As noted previously, these types of statements are well predicted by a model of decentralized administrative authority. These accounts were often made alongside specific knowledge about a court's local context, with judges, administrators, and court staff speaking about local court capacity (e.g., "We're a uniquely sized court—we're not itty-bitty, but we're not massive. We have [a number] of judges and we're self-supported as far as IT goes.

This is not always the case in [our state]. We're pretty unique in that way.") and their attentiveness to how the local conditions in their jurisdiction compared to others in the state (e.g., "I would have attorneys come back to [my jurisdiction] and be like, 'You know [being remote] has been great: I just went to [another jurisdiction] on a cattle call with thirty people and the person next to me was not wearing a mask and coughing up a storm.'"), reflecting that "completely different situations" required different types of responses. "We are not a one-size-fits-all state," remarked a court staff member in State C.

We also observe some of this activity occurring, albeit informally, in State A. Actors in State A reported how observations of the needs of people in their local jurisdictions led them to bend the rules or otherwise contravene central guidance in order to support their jurisdiction's population. Speaking about their experience with determining which hearings would be deemed "emergencies" and thus calendared during a time of restricted operations, one member of court staff in State A reflected on her experience in fielding these requests: "I noticed a large number of individuals, like, trying to work around the system. And I don't want to say I helped, but I might have facilitated [scheduling their hearings] knowing what would be heard and what wouldn't."

This type of action is not one that an analysis of administrative orders would reveal. The actor in State A describes a step she took to work within existing court policies in service of working around them: by casting a wide net around the state's definition of "emergency," she managed to calendar hearings that would not have otherwise been scheduled. She attributed this action to an acknowledgment of her local context. When speaking about a press conference held by the state's chief justice, wherein the chief was commending the response of the branch, she remarked: "The chief justice was like, 'The judicial branch never shut down.' It never shut down because of people like me. He didn't have to deal with people who were, like, sobbing. They never see these people." In this actor's view, the policies promulgated by the high court were not sensitive to local conditions. She commented that "everybody wanted the same thing; it just sometimes came at a different cost to people in some communities."

Monitoring as a Crosscutting Theme

Attentiveness to monitoring—and the central administrative apparatus's ability to force compliance if local policy actions were deemed too deviant—was present in responses as an acknowledgment of the hierarchy's ability to restrict action (most often in the case of State A) as well as of its powerlessness to do so (solely in the case of States B and C).

As was illustrated in the previous quote related to informal policy change in State A, actors in this state often reported feeling incredibly frustrated with their inability to fit policy to their local context. Even still, they tended to abide by the central office's choices for fear of sanction. In one example provided during an interview, another actor from State A was party to an operations policy deviation meant to serve her local community. It was soon caught and addressed by the central office:

> It was frustrating for us here trying to help [people on the domestic docket]. So we wanted to try and [assign people hearing dates at a time when hearings were postponed indefinitely]. The [managing] judge did speak to everybody—the court reporter, the clerk, the marshals—and said, "We're going to try and open up a little bit." Um, [the central administrator] found out and the [managing judge] got a phone call saying, "You're not allowed to do that." So we were told that we could not, you know, do that. And we have to do what we're told, because they're going to find out in the end . . . you don't have any autonomy to say, "We're suited for that."

Given interactions like these, interview subjects in State A reported very few instances of departures from the central administration's directives. It was more often the case that court actors in State A abided by decisions made at the top of the hierarchy. Occasionally, actors from State A provided examples of preempting sanctions by asking the central administration for permission to do something. One court staff member remarked, "If

we couldn't handle it, whatever it was, you know I'd reach out
[to the central office] and boom, we would have a new poster, a
new sign, a new directive . . . that was consistent with what [the
central office] was already promulgating."

In the case of States B and C, the central authority's impo-
tence was often cited as a justification for taking control and
making jurisdiction-specific policy choices about how to use
remote technologies, manage court documents, and direct the
work of remote and in-person court employees. Statements like
the following were common among judges, court staff, and administrators in these states:

> There's no consequence. You know, like, no one ever tells me,
> "Yeah, you're doing a good job at that or you're not doing a good
> job." Or anything. So if there's no consequence to you just doing
> your own thing, then yeah. You can develop, like, a really local way
> of doing your job.
>
> The only time they find out somebody's doing something
> wrong is when they read about it in the paper. I mean, I cannot tell
> you the last time a member of the administrative office was in our
> [courthouse]. We haven't had a director [from the administrative
> office] visit us in thirty years.
>
> There was nothing in the [guidance from the state supreme
> court] that said we could do that. Yeah well, there was nothing in
> [there] that said we couldn't. And that's why we did [what we did].

It was very common for actors in States B and C to perceive
little constraint in their exercise of authority, and this often was
expressed through an acknowledgment of local autonomy. Even
when guidance came from higher authorities, "people just ig-
nored it," according to one judge in State B. She went on to say
that when policies lack "teeth, you know, or enforcement—in
the end the [jurisdictions] just did what they wanted to do." Such
statements demonstrate the utility of the local control model for
explaining the behavior of implementing populations in court
systems. Actors in decentralized systems perceived a great level
of authority to sidestep high court or administrative actions. But
in spite of this recognition of the "long road to be disciplined

for noncompliance," in the words of one actor in State B, we do observe actors who share administrative preferences with high courts and those in resource-strapped jurisdictions seeking to adopt central actors' policies.

The interviews revealed that choices over case processing and court operations in state court systems involve multiple actors with varying levels of power depending on how such authority is allocated within their administrative hierarchies. In decentralized systems, court actors tend to exercise the policymaking authority allocated to them by their judiciary's organizational structure, particularly when there is a lack of existing policies or when high court guidance does not conform to their ways of working. In contrast, centralized systems tend to withhold formal policymaking authority from court actors, resulting in less formal policymaking activity. However, respondents in both systems exhibited behavior that would not be predicted by the distribution of formal authority alone, as interviewees offered evidence of the influence of factors like the political and practical utility of relying on central authority, resources provided by central actors, and the perceived lack of guidance. Administrative preference alignment and resource allocation suppressed deviant policy activity among decentralized actors, while misalignment in approaches to administration incentivized attempts to informally circumvent central orders among actors in the centralized state.

Implications for the Concentration of Administrative Power in State Court Systems

This chapter sought to provide further evidence of the value of an integrated approach to the study of the administrative choices of court actors, combining insights from a hierarchical model driven by court structure and a more diffused model of authority driven by local court context and perceived administrative distance, applying them to the work of those working in lower courts. It began by asking, if state court systems are organized administratively in more and less hierarchical ways, do lower court actors respond differently to the policies promulgated by their supreme courts? Given that the incentive and monitoring structures that we typically think of as motivating lower courts in the adjudicatory context are not as consistently present in the administrative context, I again drew from the public bureaucracy and administrative law literatures to develop an account of the circumstances under which we would expect lower court actors to comply with or defect from a supreme court's preferred implementation of a policy. Pulling from this literature, I argued that lower court actors would be responsive to the way their administrative structures empowered or constrained their behavior, but only insofar as such action conformed with their view of the high court policy's applicability to their local contexts.

Through a set of interviews with those working principally in lower courts in three states that varied according to their administrative structures, I found evidence supportive of these dynamics in the state court context. The chapter uncovered that court actors in a highly centralized court system valued centralized management of administrative choices, and that central actors monitored lower court behavior and enforced compliance when deviations from their policies were detected. However, instances of deviation still occurred when actors perceived a mismatch between local conditions and high court directives, leading lower court actors to work around the rules set by the central actors. In contrast, in more administratively decentralized states, actors acknowledge the differences in the politics and resources across jurisdictions and thus expect some level of flexibility in creating locally applicable policies. There is also a perceived lack of monitoring in these systems, which offers further flexibility to innovate locally. However, lower court actors who agreed with their supreme court's proposed operational policy solutions valued central management, as it provided political cover for locally unpopular policies, where those who disagreed valued incentives to adopt a supreme court's preferred policies, even if they would have otherwise opposed the policy had it not been accompanied by resources.

The decision to centralize or locally distinguish administrative policy in courts has important implications for how we understand the role of courts and their relationship to the populations they serve. Centralizing decision-making about court processes can provide uniformity for court users, making it easier for them to navigate their court system (Andersson, Gibson, and Lehoucq 2006). However, court systems serve diverse populations, and individual courts may have varying capacities to handle cases efficiently and effectively. Lower courts may thus benefit from having the ability to quickly adapt to the unique circumstances presented by their jurisdictional needs (e.g., Andersson and Ostrom 2008; Ayres and Braithwaite 1992). These trade-offs raise important questions about the consequences of a legal system designed to produce a more uniform model of administrative policy versus one that creates space for local adaptability. The design of these policies, and the distribution of power within a judiciary, can have a significant impact on individuals' access to justice.

Guided by evidence suggestive of the consequences of these changes for court users, the following chapter examines the longer-term impact of changes in court operations and procedures brought about by the COVID-19 pandemic. To do so, it presents the results of a survey of state-level procedural changes that have been formalized—or are in the process of being formally included—in states' civil procedural guidelines and rules of practice. These findings will demonstrate that both administratively centralized and decentralized states are discussing and formally implementing these changes, suggesting that similar, durable policy outcomes can occur across system types.

4 | Beyond Emergencies
The Influence of Power Dynamics on Administrative Policy Choices

During the COVID-19 pandemic, state supreme courts had to swiftly formulate policy responses to a rapidly unfolding crisis, managing the challenge with limited resources and information. They used a range of approaches, including the use of discretionary guidance and strict policy directives, to provide lower courts with direction on how to navigate different aspects of case processing amid stay-at-home orders and social distancing requirements. Chapter 2 proposed that the need for quick and flexible responses would prompt supreme courts with different degrees of administrative control to rely on discretionary policy tools. However, it was also suggested that in systems with more centralized administrative authority, high courts would be more likely to impose policies that limited lower courts' ability to craft policies responsive to their local environments, in spite of the considerations present in the emergency. This chapter examines state supreme courts' use of administrative authority beyond the scope of the pandemic and aims to ascertain whether the dynamics of intra-branch power observed during the pandemic were unique, or if they can also be applied to nonemergency contexts.

To do so, it compares the pandemic's emergency policymaking environment to the standard administrative policymaking processes of state courts. I draw upon the findings of the prior chapters, as well as supplemental literature from the public policy-making and civil procedure-making literatures, to offer insights about how central actors approach these decision-making processes under normal circumstances. I suggest that while the pandemic required rapid policy development, the fundamental dynamics of administrative power are durable and apply in both emergency and nonemergency conditions. The main difference between these two sets of circumstances lies in policymakers' capacity to participate in a more deliberative process during periods of calm, which enables them to contemplate various policy alternatives. Nevertheless, the possession of administrative authority remains a stable feature across both decision-making contexts.

This chapter presents evidence based on a novel data collection of proposed and codified changes to generally applicable bodies of rules including civil procedure, rules of court, and rules of judicial administration, in the states studied in chapter 2. By conducting a content analysis of prospective and codified policy changes in these states as of February 2023, I find evidence indicating a persistence of the dynamics observed during the temporary pandemic environment. In this latter period, state supreme courts tended to approve of permanent rules and procedural amendments that shared similar features with those promulgated during the pandemic period. This chapter's findings support the argument made in chapter 2, illustrating how authority over administrative tools shapes the development of both temporary and permanent policies promulgated by state supreme courts. The results also raise important questions about how these policymaking processes and their outcomes affect fairness in accessing civil courts. Depending on the style of case processing policy adopted by a state court system, people seeking to resolve their civil legal issues may have different experiences, which could lead to unequal outcomes.

The Influence of Administrative Power on Policy Adoption in and out of Emergency Circumstances

In this section, I review and further consider the literature on procedure and rulemaking processes that was previously introduced in chapters 1 and 2, with the aim of drawing comparisons between the standard processes and the circumstances of the temporary policymaking environment brought about during the pandemic. According to the works described below, policymakers responsible for crafting generally applicable administrative policies will typically incorporate features in their policy choices that reflect their level of control over the tools that enable them to execute their authority, regardless of the presence of an emergency. I explore how these insights relate to policymaking in the post-pandemic environment and assess the implications for the exercise of administrative power.

In chapter 2 I detailed the factors influencing a policymaking body's decision to distribute guidance and employ more discretionary forms of policy to regulate the entities under its purview. I argued that it would likely be beneficial for high courts to develop and circulate such policies during the pandemic, regardless of their level of practical administrative authority over lower courts. This contention stemmed from the fact that these types of policies are relatively easy to distribute and modify, particularly critical features in emergency situations like the pandemic, where swift responses were essential (Stefan 2020; see also Rocco, Béland, and Waddan 2020). The comparative procedural simplicity of disseminating advisory policies, as opposed to making changes to permanent bodies of rules and procedures, meant that even those with substantial control over their court system's operations could appreciate the ability to promptly respond with nonbinding tools.

In addition to the agility afforded by more advisory forms of policy, there may have been an information-based rationale for promulgating this style of policy. In conventional policymaking and amendment processes, high courts often have the capacity to seek advice from consultative bodies to inform changes to generally applicable administrative policies. The COVID-19 pandemic presented a complex and evolving crisis, introducing uncertainty regarding the components of the most effective response, especially given the diverse impacts on communities within states and differing views on how to respond. High courts may have deemed it more efficient to grant lower courts some decision-making power in crafting local administrative policies during the pandemic. From an informational standpoint, lower courts likely held local knowledge about the most effective pandemic response in their specific jurisdictional contexts.

By crafting policies that signaled lower courts had administrative decision-making authority, high courts mitigated the time costs associated with gathering the information needed to make more directive forms of policy.[1]

In some states, discretionary policies may have also been the primary tool available for high courts to use during the pandemic. Compared to states with more centralized forms of administration, where supreme courts and state-level administrators had access to mechanisms that facilitated the enforcement of compliance with binding policies related to case processing (see generally Behn 2001; Gormley and Balla 2004; Thierer 2021), in states where local-level actors have greater control over their operations, state-level actors may have lacked the tools necessary to enforce their preferred operations policies. As a result, state-level actors in these more decentralized states tended to design guidance materials as local actors held more control over case processing. These discretionary policies would not have the same enforceability as those binding policies distributed by central actors with greater administrative authority, but as demonstrated in chapter 3, still had a meaningful impact on choices made at the local level (Thierer 2021; Bardach and Kagan 1982; see also Snyder 1994).

The pandemic underscored the utilization of discretionary policy language in states where technology-related functions were managed in a decentralized way, as illustrated by the Michigan Supreme Court's approach to crafting operations policies. Unlike states with centralized management of electronic filing systems, such as New Hampshire and Vermont, Michigan had not yet implemented a uniform system that would allow for statewide binding policy changes related to methods of document filing—lower courts retained significant autonomy in deciding how to manage case filings and document submissions within their jurisdictions.[2] Consequently, state-level actors in Michigan could not require lower courts to follow a mandatory policy that reflected the Court's preferred case processing modifications during the pandemic. Instead, the Court crafted case processing guidelines with local-level autonomy as a guiding principle. The Michigan Supreme Court's guidance on case filing during the pandemic proposed a variety of alternatives to in-person filing, including the MIfile electronic filing platform, which was used in a handful of jurisdictions before the pandemic. The Court also encouraged the use of physical drop boxes, postal mail, e-mail, and fax for filings. According to a Michigan Supreme Court working group document, jurisdictions took advantage of a wide range of methods that varied in the degree to which they utilized technology. The Michigan report further underscored the interplay between a decentralized administrative structure and the resulting local-level variation, noting that even within some jurisdictions individual judges took different approaches, including some who refused to accept electronic filings as an alternative altogether.[3]

In contrast to the emergency environment, in standard administrative policy change processes, policymakers may have more time and resources to gather information, permitting them to consider their options and test policy alternatives. Under "normal" conditions, rule- and procedure-making in state courts and the federal system alike is a deliberative process that typically happens in a routinized way within a court system (see generally Clopton 2018, appendixes A, B; see also Breyer 1996).[4] As described in chapter 1, in states where court systems hold the primary authority to make these policies, the processes to consider new or revised policies are typically initiated by supreme courts themselves or through the activities of advisory committees or formal policymaking bodies within court systems. These bodies may use pilot programs to address administrative reform proposals that are particularly complex. Proposals may also come directly from lower courts, and in some states the public participates through the notice and comment process. Although there are idiosyncrasies that make state systems different, the process is usually highly centralized when managed by state supreme courts.[5]

As the pandemic emergency subsides, supreme courts can now engage in a more deliberative process, enabling them to collect information and consider policy alternatives. While the presence of an emergency led high courts to widely employ discretionary policies for their convenience and flexibility, differences in the concentration of administrative power in high courts should be durable and result in variation in their adoption of discretionary or more binding types of policies in a non-emergency context.

An Examination of Policies Adopted by State Supreme Courts Post-Pandemic

The following analysis considers whether the characteristics of policies promulgated during the pandemic are similar to or different from those formulated in the post-pandemic period, taking into account the durability of the underlying sources of authority held by supreme courts. Specifically, I focus on a subset of technology-related proposals and enactments concerning the management and exchange of documents and participation in hearings in the most administratively centralized and decentralized states discussed in chapter 2. This categorization is augmented with information about rulemaking processes from Clopton (2018) and is illustrated in table 4.1. Using these changes as indicators of policy activity within specific areas of case processing facilitates a cross-state comparison outside of the emergency context.[6]

Examining these categories of technology-related policies enables a relatively comprehensive exploration of the types of policy changes proposed and adopted in state court systems for use in the post-pandemic period, while also narrowing the scope of inquiry. During this period, court systems also considered proposals to change other rules and processes unrelated to technology. Although such proposals are also meaningful in terms of modifying aspects of how cases are processed, they are less likely to have originated from or been spurred along by courts' responses to the pandemic. I also account for changes made throughout the entire study period due to courts' use of distinct cycles for evaluating and adopting rules (see, e.g., Clopton 2018). Even though few technology-related rules were made permanent in the earliest part of the study period, the timing of

Table 4.1. States by Remote-Relevant Administrative Centralization Score Quartile with Clopton (2018) Categories

Lower 25%	50th Percentile	Upper 25%
Florida,[a] **Indiana**, *Louisiana*,[b] **Michigan**, **Missouri**, **Nevada**, **Ohio**, Pennsylvania, South Carolina, **Texas**, Washington[c]	Alaska, Arizona, *California*, Delaware, *Georgia*, *Illinois*, Iowa, *Kansas*, Maryland, Minnesota, Mississippi, New Jersey, New Mexico, *North Carolina*, North Dakota, Oregon, South Dakota, Tennessee,[d] Utah, Wisconsin	**Alabama**, **Arkansas**, Colorado, *Connecticut*, **Hawai`i**, **Kentucky**, **Massachusetts**, New Hampshire, **Rhode Island**, **Vermont**, West Virginia

[a] **Bold** indicates a state that is included in the document analysis. States that did not submit responses to the NCSC SCO survey are ID, ME, MT, NE, NY, OK, VA, and WY.

[b] *Italics* indicates a state wherein the legislature is principally responsible for promulgating civil procedure (Clopton 2018).

[c] While scoring within the 25th percentile, Washington is the only state in this group with an authority that was centrally controlled.

[d] While scoring above the 25th percentile, Tennessee is the only state in the middle 50% that has at least one locally controlled administrative authority and no centrally controlled authorities.

opportunities to consider policy changes varies by court system, necessitating consideration of the entire period.

I collected evidence of policy changes made by court systems that stemmed directly from the courts' pandemic-era experiences with specific forms of temporary procedural modifications, as well as of those permanent changes that could not be directly attributed to a specific temporary alteration. I took this approach because of the wide variation in the content of emergency orders, in terms of the topics covered and the specificity with which they were covered. For example, some supreme courts gave lower courts flexibility in making determinations about how to handle aspects of the virtual environment, which could have been specific, like Vermont's removal of barriers to allow for service of process via e-mail,[7] or general, such as Florida's Supreme Court's extension of discretion to presiding judges to make choices they deemed necessary to respond to the challenges presented by the pandemic.[8] In the latter case, the Florida Supreme Court may not have been specific about how courts were to apply technology; instead, the Court presented lower courts with an opportunity to innovate across a variety of steps of case processing. Lower courts in turn may have formally acknowledged their specific activities in response, but as described in chapter 3, they may have also practiced them informally. Therefore, connecting a specific temporary policy provision to its permanent counterpart may be an underinclusive approach for this analysis.

The pandemic also prompted modifications to court processes that were already being considered for implementation by courts, and I have incorporated these changes into my analysis. A number of states have explained in their commentaries accompanying their policy changes that the pandemic era accelerated the adoption of policies that were being considered for implementation over a longer time frame. For example, Vermont and New Jersey accelerated their adoption of a statewide e-filing system, and Michigan refined its approach given courts' experiences with multiple modalities of document filing during the pandemic.[9] I acknowledge these instances when applicable in the following analysis.

During the study period, the selected states promulgated over 110 documents containing over 230 versions of pending or approved modifications to existing bodies of administrative rules and procedures, as well as completely novel policies, related to the integration of technological advancements in civil court proceedings. These documents were collected through a review of administrative policy change-related documents promulgated by state court systems on their websites. Although these documents were typically found on webpages where supreme courts promulgate pending and approved changes to such policies, they were also found on pages that detailed the work of rule- and procedure-making committees and those that provide press releases and news alerts about a court system's work. Although most court-promulgated documents contained the full content of a policy change, including additions to text, the content that was removed, and commentary useful for understanding the change in context, this was not always the case. Therefore, I also collected and reviewed supplemental, external sources of data, such as commentary published by state bar associations and the text of former iterations of administrative policies found in prior editions of states' rules and procedural publications to capture contextual factors that may have been overlooked in documents approving specific changes.

My review of the technology-related permanent procedural changes enacted or pending in the study states revealed that these changes were implemented or under consideration at the statewide level in states across the administrative centralization spectrum. However, characteristics of these policies tended to differ according to a judiciary's distinct method of distributing administrative power. State supreme courts working in systems with more centralized administrative structures tended to enact policies offering limited discretion to lower courts, whereas those with more decentralized structures tended to develop more flexible policies, with some exceptions to this trend. Overall, the results suggest that courts operating under different intra-branch power arrangements can establish technology-related policies, but the level of administrative authority held by central actors plays a crucial role in shaping policy content, both during and outside of emergency circumstances.

Control over Technological Tools and Electronic Document Management Policies

As highlighted in the examples advanced in chapter 2 and touched on earlier in this chapter, state court systems faced the challenge of managing document filing and exchange while limiting in-person interactions during the pandemic period. In states with centralized or widely accessible e-filing systems, state supreme courts tended to disseminate policies that demonstrated control over the options lower courts had for transitioning to a fully remote environment. In states without such systems in place, state supreme courts tended to provide suggested best practices to lower courts as to how they should manage document submission and distribution. As court systems entered the post-pandemic period, states with more and less centralized administrative structures implemented procedural changes to expand access to e-filing for a wider range of civil case types, geographic jurisdictions, and parties. They also made modifications that signaled changes in the methods of filing that people were more commonly using, with Vermont removing barriers to efficient processing of electronically filed documents, and Florida acknowledging that a close of business standard was unnecessary for electronically filed documents.[10]

Courts have not only adopted alternative methods for filing documents and modified related operational policies but have also established new policies concerning service of process. These policies include expanding the acceptable methods of service of process and developing new requirements for notifying courts of successful service. *Service of process* is the formal way in which parties communicate across multiple stages of a civil case, including its initiation, the discovery phase, the exchange of pre-trial motions, and potentially the issuance of subpoenas for witnesses and additional documents if a case goes to trial. Traditionally, service of process is done in person through a delegated authority (e.g., a sheriff or a process server), physical mail, or via news publication. However, some courts were already experimenting with an expanded set of alternative methods before the pandemic, such as via social media or e-mail.[11] During the pandemic, more courts tried out electronic service options like these. These alternatives were designed within permissive formal procedural rules (in that they allowed for alternative methods of service without specifically naming electronic methods) or through temporary orders designed to explicitly sanction them. Further, while some courts had also incorporated electronic methods of notification that service had been completed before the pandemic period, courts expanded their use of such methods during this time.

State court systems with decentralized administrative arms tended to make changes to procedural language regarding the methods of completing service during the period analyzed; states with more centralized administrative bodies focused their policy changes more on the development of methods for notifying courts that service had been successfully effectuated. In other words, both types of systems were crafting policy relevant to service of process, but their approaches to crafting policies were related to different components of service. Policy changes in state courts with more centralized administrations likely took advantage of electronic filing systems that incorporated electronic forms of notifying courts of successful service attempts, while more decentralized administrative systems used procedural changes related to service of process to expand the options available for acceptable methods of conducting service. These differences illustrate the importance of centralized administrative control in enabling courts to make uniform changes to procedures related to technology. A comparison of Vermont's approach to codifying new e-service rules with the changes in Michigan, Indiana, Ohio, and Florida provides useful insights.

In the state of Vermont, a series of rules changes and proposed changes have sought (and seek, in the case of rules changes that were pending at the end of the analysis period) to modernize and transition the court system to the electronic environment. In April 2020, Vermont began a broad rollout of a new electronic filing system. Although electronic filing had been used in the Vermont courts since 2010, it was used in a more limited number of courts and dockets.[12] The codification of a new set of electronic filing rules in July 2020 signaled a shift in Vermont's approach to the use of technology in different stages of case processing.[13] Since the adoption of the new rules and a new case management and e-filing system (Odyssey), the Vermont Supreme Court has codified a number of rules changes both supportive of and dependent on the statewide rollout of this system.

For example, in 2021 and 2022 several rule amendments

were implemented to modernize the court system's electronic filing procedures. These amendments aimed to clarify the process of obtaining evidence that the opposing party received a document, as well as the requirements for serving legal documents in general and for serving documents related to discovery in particular. There were also smaller technical changes—for example, mentions of "papers" were changed to "documents" in Vermont's civil procedural rules in acknowledgment of the fact that physical paper was not the only vehicle for transmitting a document.[14] Notably, these rules changes have acknowledged that their effectuation was predicated on the entire judiciary's transition to the Odyssey system.[15] As such, we can consider these changes as standardizing service-related procedures, making these rules and requirements broadly applicable to all courts throughout the state's system, while also allowing a limited amount of discretion for judicial officers to determine acceptable modes of filing in their respective courts.

Ohio's approach to modifying its service of process rules differs from Vermont's, possibly due to the lack of centralized control over relevant administrative tools. In Vermont, the court system utilizes a centrally administered electronic filing system. In contrast, Ohio does not have a centrally managed document filing system, leading to interjurisdictional variability as central actors in Ohio have limited control over this aspect of case management. Consequently, many jurisdictions in Ohio use a case management system with e-filing capabilities developed by an outside software company, while others have created their own in-house systems for use of their individual courts alone. Courts utilizing varied case management systems may thus not offer the full range of court services electronically, or they may not provide electronic service options for all case types authorized by law, due to variations in their systems' capabilities to do so. For instance, a court may allow the electronic submission of documents for a new civil case filing but not permit parties to use the e-filing system to certify service of process.[16]

Due to differences in administrative tools available to high courts across these systems, it is unlikely that the Ohio Supreme Court would adopt permanent rule changes similar to those approved by the Vermont Supreme Court in the post-pandemic period. A look at the Ohio Supreme Court's amendments to the system's service of process rules, which went into effect in July 2022, is instructive. While the updated rule allows for service to be completed via fax or e-mail, the commentary accompanying the change pointed out that there was no deadline stipulated for lower courts to adopt this rule while simultaneously stressing that transitioning to accepting electronic process "should be a priority for all courts."[17] Similarly, Michigan's Supreme Court, which faces similar challenges as Ohio with variations in approaches to filing used across the state court system, updated the system's service of process rules to acknowledge that electronic means "must be performed" for service across most stages of document exchange.[18] Recognizing the lack of control over individual courts' choices, the rule change recommends that courts adopt these methods "to the greatest extent possible."[19]

Ohio and Michigan's recent updates to their service of process rules demonstrate both their acknowledgment of the advantages of electronic filing and their efforts to modernize court procedures within their policy-making capacity. Ohio and Michigan are unlikely to adopt Vermont's model of a uniform approach to service of process given their inability to enforce the application of such rules. Instead, expanding the acceptable methods of service of process may be a more appropriate approach given their administrative constraints.

In other states lacking centralized management of electronic filing, like Florida and Indiana, changes similar to those in Ohio and Michigan have been made regarding acceptable methods of service. In these states, the service of process methods have been extended to include "any other means" beyond those explicitly stated in the rule.[20] These changes in service rules indicate a trend toward the acceptance of a broader range of alternative methods of service, while still allowing individual courts to exercise discretion in determining which methods they will use.

During the studied period, most updates to service of process rules in the examined states occurred in the bodies of rules and procedures in decentralized systems. In contrast, permanent changes to methods of gathering information about completed service were predominantly observed in centralized systems. While the nature of these changes highlight the contrast in approaches between states with centralized and decentralized administrative power, policy changes in the administratively decentralized states also included language affirming the role of state-level court actors in decision-making. For example, in both Indiana and Ohio, state court administrators are stipulated as the people who are responsible for making determinations about the types of electronic service methods that are deemed acceptable within the scope of the revised policy.[21] As another example, rule changes in both Texas and Florida acknowledge explicit examples of why electronic service of process might not be an acceptable method to communicate with a party, with unreliable access to technology as a key factor in making such a determination.[22]

Changes to Communication Policies Emanating from Pre-Pandemic and External Initiatives

While acknowledging the significance of the aforementioned changes, it is also important to note that not all modifications to court processes were internally driven, nor were they exclusively intended to address the lessons learned during the pandemic. During the pandemic, state supreme courts frequently emphasized the limitations of their authority in altering court procedures. In their temporary orders, they often added that any modifications courts in their systems made—both at the state and local levels—would need to be consistent with existing statutory and constitutional requirements. Given that courts do not operate in isolation from these external policy considerations, aside from any self-initiated efforts by courts to update their rules, the introduction of new and amended statutes may necessitate a reevaluation of internal rules and procedures. In certain states, statutory requirements also evolved to respond to the lessons of the pandemic. As a consequence, courts were compelled to contemplate rules changes that aligned with these legislative adoptions.

For example, in June 2022 the Florida Legislature passed updates to the Florida Statutes that allowed for expanded methods of service of process, including a range of electronic methods, for certain types of parties.[23] This change (among other legislative actions) led the Florida Supreme Court to refer the matter to the civil procedure committee of the Florida State Bar Association, a standing committee that advises the Court's civil rulemaking process (see also Clopton 2018).[24] In its response to the Court, the committee proposed a change to the Court's rules governing service of process. The rules change was approved by the Court shortly after the statutory change took effect. While the change to the rule resulted from an internal court process, the Court's consideration of such an amendment arose from changes in state laws that the Court deemed as potentially impacting court processes.

Procedural innovations that were implemented in *response* to state courts' pandemic experiences were not the only changes being discussed in these systems during the study period. Prior to the pandemic, there were already ongoing conversations about broader process reforms, and some of the innovations that were ultimately adopted in the post-pandemic period had been part of these discussions. For example, the Hawai`i Supreme Court promulgated a series of permanent revisions to civil court forms during the study period—including the inclusion of a space for parties' e-mail addresses—but these court forms were revised as part of a much longer-term project mounted by the Civil Justice Improvements Task Force established by the Supreme Court in 2018.[25] The task force also recommended the inclusion of e-mail addresses in other court-based processes, like its proposed change to Hawai`i's Circuit Court Rules requiring self-represented litigants to provide clerks with their e-mail addresses (in addition to other contact information).[26] While the rollout of these revised forms was underway during the pandemic, the Hawai`i Supreme Court acknowledged that the pandemic experience led to systemwide reflections on other components of the task force's recommendations, changing the Court's outlook on adopting other procedural changes. With that said, we also have direct evidence that changes to court forms did directly emanate from the pandemic experience. For example, during the pandemic, a task force established by the Ohio Supreme Court recommended a series of changes to the state's rules of civil procedure, including the requirement to obtain e-mail addresses as part of the discovery process if a party maintained one.[27] The Ohio Supreme Court considered and eventually adopted these recommendations, which directly resulted from the pandemic experience.[28]

Although many permanent changes to court procedures regarding communication of court information during the pandemic resulted from internal court processes that addressed lessons learned, others were influenced by pre-pandemic reform projects or shifts in statutory requirements. Generally speaking, these changes indicate the level of procedural control exerted by central actors over the procedural choices made by lower courts. In administratively centralized states, policy changes related to court communication tended to be linked to changes in court forms and certification of service, while in more administratively decentralized states, there were expansions of acceptable methods of service of process. These changes emphasize the importance of a state's control over administrative tools, such as electronic filing systems or the design of court forms, in the development of uniform policies regarding the exchange of documents and formal communication between courts and parties.

Managing Judicial Discretion over Choices of Hearing Modality in More and Less Administratively Centralized Systems

The pandemic also posed a major challenge for court systems in managing participation during trials and other types of court hearings. As acknowledged in this book's introductory chapter, some states had prior experience using videoconferencing technology for pre-trial hearings in civil matters and across hearing types in criminal matters, but the pandemic required court systems to develop plans to use remote communication technologies for a broader range of hearings. Supreme courts and state-level administrators took varying approaches in managing this component of pandemic response, leading to a patchwork of technology usage both within and across states. Some of these policies were top-down choices that placed greater constraint on lower courts, while others delegated considerable authority to lower courts to make choices about the types of cases and circumstances under which remote or in-person participation in hearings would be required or most appropriate.

State supreme court chief justices across the country have since spoken about the importance of making remote access to court proceedings permanently available after the end of the public health emergency.[29] However, codifying rules related to remote appearances in hearings presents challenges, particularly in administratively decentralized systems where lower courts have greater autonomy in their choices about their day-to-day operations and how they process cases. As a consequence, we would expect to see variation in the language used in permanent enactments, with supreme courts in more administratively decentralized systems offering greater discretion to permit hearings to occur across modalities. While the majority of changes observed during the study period across the study states included language codifying judicial discretion and outlining circumstances permitting exceptions to the rules, there was variability in how these enactments described other aspects of the remote environment. For example, court systems with more centralized administrative arms tended to stipulate specific case types that would be held presumptively remote or in person. In contrast, supreme courts in states where there was more administrative decentralization offered broader categorizations allowing for greater flexibility. Such additional specifications in the former case suggest fewer opportunities for judges and others working in courts to exercise discretion. Variation in the scope of discretion manifested in other ways as well, and tended to reflect the level of control high courts maintain over the administrative aspects of case processing. These features are described in more detail below.

In the study states, pre-pandemic rules regarding hearing

modality typically granted judges the discretion to determine whether participants could join certain types of hearings using specific technologies, provided that courts had established such rules. Changes that have emanated from the pandemic experience within the study period often required wholesale revisions of existing procedures, across both more and less administratively centralized states. For example, the pre-revision language in Vermont's rules of small claims procedure pertaining to hearing modality in nonjury hearings reads as follows:

> (2) *Conduct of Hearing.*
> (A) Upon motion in a non-jury hearing, participation of a party or testimony of a witness may be allowed by telephone in the judge's discretion.

In a 2022 revision,[30] this language was entirely deleted and replaced with the following:

> (2) *Conduct of Hearing.*
> (A) In a nonjury hearing, the court may preside by remote audio or video and require all parties, witnesses, counsel, and other persons to participate by remote audio or video. In advance of the hearing date, participants may request an in-person hearing based on the relevant factors in V.R.C.P. 43.1.[31] The court may grant an in-person hearing based on a consideration of the relevant factors.

The unrevised version of this provision is fairly restrictive as compared to the revised version. The former offers the opportunity for parties to participate in hearings by telephone, but only by their request and with a judge's subsequent approval of it. In addition to the general increase in the space dedicated to explaining the use of communication technologies in hearings, the new version of the rule suggests that remote participation is the default in small claims hearings, with the option for in-person participation upon request and a judge's consideration of factors relevant to making such a determination.

Similarly, Florida's rules of practice and litigation procedures previously dedicated less space to articulating the uses of remote communication technology in the courtroom, with a former version of Rule 2.530 stipulating that trial court judges at the county and circuit levels could utilize communication equipment for motion hearings, pre-trial conferences, or status conferences upon the written request of a party or upon their own motion.[32] This version of the rule also stipulated that judges were authorized to utilize communication equipment over parties' objections in many circumstances. In contrast, the 2022 revision to the rule is considerably broader in its description of acceptable uses of communication technologies, permitting their use across all civil court proceedings (except civil proceedings for involuntary commitment), subject to certain conditions and with consideration of potential objections parties may raise.

CODIFYING JUDICIAL DISCRETION IN DETERMINATIONS OF HEARING MODALITY, WITH VARIED LIMITATIONS

During the study period, in most cases where courts made changes to their rules regarding participation in hearings, judges have been delegated the power to determine the modality of the proceeding, whether it is entirely in-person, a hybrid format, or entirely online. Generally, new and revised provisions give judges discretion over whether parties or other hearing participants can appear using a modality that is not the presumptive type of participation for a given case. To illustrate, some rule changes have classified hearings in a binary way, specifying that some broad categories of hearing types, such as those involving the presentation of evidence or testimony or the presence of a jury, should be presumed to be held in person, while hearings not falling into these categories should be presumed to be held remotely.[33] This type of binary categorization is present in rules changes across states with varying degrees of administrative centralization. These new enactments and amendments to existing rules allow parties to request a change in modality for their participation, but judges retain the authority to deny such requests or to overrule objections to judges' determinations of modality.[34]

Some supreme courts have taken categorization a step further, articulating in their rules detailed lists of specific types of cases that should be heard using a particular modality—above and beyond the dual categorization examples given above. Giving more detailed information about the types of cases that should presumptively be heard in a particular modality could be perceived as placing a greater level of constraint on judges than the dual category approach.

These additional specifications were more commonly observed in the more administratively centralized states but were not limited to them. For example, Hawai`i, a more administratively centralized state, changed its rule regarding appearances by telephone or video to include such specifications for circumstances under which appearing remotely was presumptively allowed (e.g., uncontested motions, trial-setting conferences, status conferences) and where it was not presumptively allowed (e.g., contested motions, settlement conferences, trials).[35] Through the adoption of a permanent standing order applying to all superior courts, the more centralized Massachusetts took a similar approach in its post-pandemic rulemaking, specifying even more categories for presumptively remote (e.g., motions to dismiss, discovery disputes, case management conferences) and in-person hearings (e.g., injunction hearings, motions for summary judgment).[36] However, we also observe such specifications in more decentralized states, like in Florida, where a revision of the court system's rule on the use of technology in hearings now states that "court official[s] must grant a motion to use communication technology for a non-evidentiary court proceeding scheduled for 30 minutes or less," though the judge may still deny the request for good cause.[37]

INTERPRETING THE NATURE OF LIMITATIONS ON JUDICIAL DISCRETION IN DETERMINING HEARING MODALITY

In spite of language acknowledging judicial discretion appearing in all enactments analyzed during the study period, judges may perceive provisions with additional stipulations as either limiting or empowering their behavior. This distinction is particularly notable in states where supreme courts offered significant grants of discretion to judges to make decisions regarding how they would hold hearings during the pandemic. On one hand, judges who disagree with the categorizations set forth by the rule may find that contesting it through overruling party requests will consume time and effort, decreasing their overall efficiency. On the other hand, some judges may employ such provisions as an easier way to reject party requests for an alternative modality if they prefer holding hearings in the way presumed by the rule.

The dynamics of how specifying additional case types of a presumptive hearing modality can be perceived as constraining can be seen in Michigan's case. Despite being a more administratively decentralized state, Michigan codified a list of presumptively remote civil hearing types upon the recommendation of its Lessons Learned Committee. The revised provision allows courts to utilize videoconferencing technology in civil proceedings, either upon a party's request or at their own discretion. However, this technology cannot be used in bench or jury trials, or in civil proceedings that involve witness testimony or evidence presentation, unless all parties have been notified and given the opportunity to be heard.[38] The provision also lists various specific hearing types, such as civil pre-trials and post-judgment collection and discovery matters, as examples of presumptively remote hearings in both district and circuit courts. Two justices dissented from the order promulgating these provisions, with one justice reasoning that the provision stripped trial courts of discretion in deciding how to best conduct remote proceedings. In response, Chief Justice McCormack clarified in the Court's majority opinion that the amendments did not require judges to adhere to a remote option in cases where it would be inappropriate or undesirable for a participant, adding that the new rules did not strip trial courts of their discretion in making determinations of hearing modality.[39]

In another example, at the recommendation of its Remote Proceeding Task Force, the Texas Supreme Court codified a method of evaluating good cause arguments raised in parties' objections to a hearing modality that could either be viewed as creating efficiencies for judges and permitting them flexibility in exercising their discretion or as constraining their ability to act independently. In its amendment to a procedural rule regarding remote participation, the Court approved of the inclusion of a list that specifies considerations judges should keep in mind when assessing a party's good cause rationale for objecting to a hearing modality.[40] The list could be viewed as either constraining judges or creating efficiencies in their exercise of discretion, depending on one's perspective. Without such a list, the task force reasoned that judges may have been able to develop their own locally applicable considerations through their decisions in cases, while having a list could allow judges to rely upon it in their evaluation of a participant's ability to fully engage in a hearing using a certain modality, creating efficiencies in their evaluations and some degree of consistency within and across jurisdictions.

State supreme courts and central administrators have taken varying approaches to codifying post-pandemic hearing modality rules. Changes to generally applicable bodies of rules often required significant revisions of existing procedures, in both more and less administratively centralized states. In most cases where courts have made changes to their rules regarding participation in hearings, judges have been granted the power to make final determinations about the modality of participation in hearings. Despite this flexibility, codifying rules related to remote appearances in hearings has been challenging, particularly in administratively decentralized systems where lower courts have greater autonomy over their day-to-day operations and case processing methods.

The Broader Applicability of the Concentration of Administrative Power on Policy Outcomes in State Court Systems

This chapter sought to assess the applicability of the administrative power distribution explanation of supreme courts' case processing and operational policy choices in chapter 2 to a nonemergency context. It began with an examination of the differences in the considerations state supreme courts may be mindful of in emergency and nonemergency contexts and concluded that the major difference presented in the nonemergency context is that a court's normal policymaking process offers more opportunities for deliberation and systematic forms of information seeking. Given that the types of tools state supreme courts have control over are likely to remain stable across emergency and nonemergency periods, I suggested that we should see similar types of features—notably, the use of more or less discretionary forms of policy language—according to the degree of control state supreme courts have over the practical tools that can ensure lower courts' compliance with their preferred policy outcomes, regardless of the presence or absence of an emergency situation.

This analysis reviewed proposed and approved changes as well as new additions to the generally applicable rules of courts from April 2020 to February 2023. The findings suggest that supreme courts have tended to adopt permanent policies with similar features to those temporary policies that they designed and promulgated during the pandemic. This supports the argument made in chapter 2, with some exceptions that are reviewed below. In the case of electronic document processing, states with centralized e-filing tended to advance policies that reflected the fact that they have more control over lower courts' transition to remote environments, while states without such systems tended to suggest best practices and guidance supportive of their preferred approaches to the transition. The remote hearing policies permanently incorporated into court rules and procedures by state supreme courts within the time period analyzed generally reflect the approaches they took to managing the remote environment during the pandemic. States that exerted greater control over decisions about hearing modalities during the pandemic generally established more defined policies for the use of technology in post-pandemic hearings. In contrast, states that granted lower courts more flexibility in determining modalities during the pandemic typically allowed courts to continue making those choices in the post-pandemic period, although there were some exceptions.

With respect to the exceptions, I noted that stakeholder

groups played a vital role in discussing and promoting policy solutions. The policy recommendations put forward by these groups were either supported and acknowledged by supreme court majorities during the rulemaking process or explained in reports that detailed how the groups' deliberations led to the proposal of specific rules. The degree of centralization of administrative authority is undoubtedly a critical factor for understanding the features of policies that have been approved of by state supreme courts. But when state supreme courts intend to modify broadly applicable rules and procedures, examples like those from both more decentralized systems like Texas and Michigan and more centralized systems like Vermont demonstrate an important feature of many court systems' rulemaking processes: high courts typically seek advice and recommendations from an external body at some point in the process. The pandemic experience led court systems to reconsider a wide range of extant rules and procedures, and many stakeholders were impacted by the short-term policies implemented during this period. This has led to a significant expansion in the diversity of perspectives from which state supreme courts could seek advice during the rulemaking process.

These observations bring to mind the insights gained in the interviews with lower court actors as described in chapter 3. According to some actors, when they felt included in their supreme courts' decision-making processes in the temporary policy environment, they tended to be more supportive of their high courts' policy choices. Soliciting feedback and recommendations from implementers and other stakeholders during the pandemic likely played a crucial role in generating support for emergency measures, regardless of whether they were binding or nonbinding. The concluding chapter builds on this theme, as well as other threads from throughout the book, to examine how state supreme courts took advantage of opportunities to engage with these additional perspectives in the post-pandemic period. It also provides insights into the ramifications of doing so, or failing to do so, for the legitimacy of the processes and the level of support for resulting policies.

The findings of this chapter also prompt a discussion of the concerns raised about the accessibility of courts as described in the introductory chapter. The evidence offered here suggests that a court system's administrative framework is relevant to its approach to handling the construction of procedural language. The outcomes of procedural change can either hinder or enhance the average court user's ability to successfully navigate judicial institutions. As such, scholars and courts should also be mindful of possible variations in user experience stemming from both the types of procedural changes courts have put into practice and the way in which the language of these changes aligns with implementation strategies. These considerations are further discussed in the concluding chapter.

Conclusion
Power Dynamics and Administrative Capacity: Directions for Future Research and Implications for State Court Systems

The ability to make policy decisions in court systems extends beyond high courts and is not solely exercised through appellate power. While a hierarchical framework is useful for structuring our thinking about how court systems are organized administratively and how they operate, it is also important to acknowledge that it should be carefully applied to the choices court systems make in the administrative realm. The administrative choices of state courts, which are often made outside of the adjudicatory context, are not necessarily subject to correction via monitoring mechanisms and are not always accompanied by incentives or threats that would encourage lower court actors to align their court operations with the preferences of their supreme courts.

The main goal of the book was to offer a nuanced account of the exercise of administrative power within state court systems. To achieve this objective, I investigated the hierarchical dynamics and local factors that collectively shape the strength of central actors and influence how lower courts respond to the authority of high courts. In this chapter I offer a brief summary of the book's main contributions, reflect on its role in advancing theoretical understanding of how administrative power is distributed within in court systems, explore additional avenues for extending its empirical efforts, and assess its impacts on both courts and the people they serve.

Understanding Administrative Power in State Court Systems

After establishing the differences between the sources of administrative power within state court systems, this book delved into the logic of how hierarchical and local dynamics interrelate through a series of empirical exercises. First, it investigated whether state supreme courts in more administratively centralized court systems made distinct choices regarding how to direct court operations during the pandemic as compared to their counterparts overseeing more administratively decentralized systems. I introduced an approach to measuring administrative centralization, relying on a subset of administrative powers I deemed most relevant to the technology-related policy choices central to the study, and assessed the approaches adopted by supreme courts across these system types. The analysis revealed that the extent of administrative capacity held by central actors tended to manifest in the features of the policies promulgated by high courts during the initial stages of the pandemic.

The study proceeded with an investigation of the response of lower court personnel to the policies established by supreme courts in states with varying degrees of administrative centralization. The different tools accessible to high courts to encourage or compel compliance among lower courts imply that central actors have differing capacities to ensure the faithful implementation of their preferred operational policies. To gain deeper insights into this matter, I conducted interviews with individuals working in lower courts in both more and less administratively centralized states. The interviews indicated that when high courts employ incentives to encourage compliance, lower court personnel in decentralized states are more likely to follow their lead compared to situations where incentives are absent. Conversely, in the absence of incentives in decentralized systems, lower court actors may feel more strongly influenced by their local circumstances, resulting in the formulation of locally applicable policies. Those operating in administratively centralized systems usually reported adherence to their high court's directives due to a perceived obligation to do so, but there were exceptions. These findings suggest that even in centralized systems, local context may still hold significant weight if actors perceive that it diverges from what central mandates require.

In its final exercise, the book explored whether its core argument applied beyond emergency situations such as the COVID-19 pandemic. While the need for rapid decision-making during a crisis may alter the considerations that high court actors must keep in mind when devising operational policies for their systems, the underlying power structures that shape the capacity to perform administrative authority should remain present across emergency and nonemergency contexts. To investigate this further, I compared the policies under consideration or formally approved for incorporation into state court systems' bodies of generally applicable rules and procedures with the temporary policies issued by the same states' supreme courts during the pandemic. The findings revealed that the policies made permanent for the post-pandemic period retained features like those that states with more or less centralized administrative systems employed during the pandemic. In essence, the choices made by state supreme courts regarding case processing and operational policies tended to reflect the concentration of administrative power in their systems, providing evidence of the applicability of the book's central argument beyond the pandemic context.

Implications for Researchers: Advancing Theory and Extending the Empirical Framework

This book leveraged the surge of policy activity in courts brought about by the COVID-19 pandemic to explore the relationship between administrative policy dynamics in state court systems, the operational policies crafted by state supreme courts, and the decisions lower court actors make regarding implementation. The empirical chapters revealed insights about court organization, how those working within court systems make calculations regarding the scope of their authority, and the impacts of these dynamics on the design and implementation of administrative policies.

These findings motivate several complementary research endeavors, including those aimed at advancing a theoretical account of these dynamics in addition to those utilizing the existing empirical framework to conduct further investigations of technology-driven procedural change within court systems. Moreover, the findings prompt a broader discussion about how we might approach conducting research on administrative power in courts in the future, which requires an acknowledgment of what makes this research endeavor distinct from how we study adjudicatory power. This section discusses each of these opportunities in turn.

Developing a Theory of Administrative Power Dynamics in State Court Systems

This study has examined indicators of both structural constraint and behavioral dynamics pertinent to understanding the exercise of administrative power in state courts. However, it is important to emphasize that only a subset of the range of possible indicators were explored in this empirical project. Scholars could identify and investigate additional indicators, contributing to further development of a theory of administrative power in state court systems. In the context of structural constraints, limitations on (or the empowerment of) administrative authority in judiciaries could stem from institutional structures beyond those that assign authority over specific administrative tools within court systems. In terms of lower court actors' behavior and perspectives on implementation, there is room for additional investigation of indicators that shed light on determinants of compliance and faithful implementation.

Here, I propose additional indicators aimed at enhancing our understanding of administrative decision-making in courts, focusing on those that emerge from the two primary categories central to this project. First, I introduce another indicator derived from the structural component of the argument and propose a study of how the policies originating outside of the judicial branch can impact the subsequent exercise of administrative power by court actors. Then, I explore a possible examination of the durability and legitimacy of procedural change within court systems, considering patterns of information-seeking in the stages of these policymaking processes. Through these efforts, I seek to motivate additional scholarly dialogue focused on advancing a comprehensive theoretical account of these dynamics.

INTER-BRANCH DYNAMICS AND THE ADMINISTRATIVE CAPACITY OF STATE COURT ACTORS

In this book, and particularly in chapter 2, I acknowledged how policy changes external to state court systems can affect court actors' ability to exercise their administrative powers. Executive and legislative actions at the state and federal levels can significantly influence how state court actors approach their administrative roles. The choices made by other branches of government can require state courts to adjust their procedures or even develop entirely new processes. This can lead to variations in how state courts approach similar policy issues (e.g., Arbuthnot 2002; see also Tobin and Hudzik 1993). This section illustrates an area that would benefit from further study: the connection between policy activity external to the judicial branch and the subsequent development and execution of administrative policies that regulate court operations. By examining these inter-branch dynamics, we can expand on the argument presented in this book and highlight how external actors can either empower or restrict the administrative actions of state court actors.

The response of state courts to the eviction crisis exacerbated by the pandemic offers a chance to investigate how state courts modified their procedures and how this variation relates to policy choices made by external actors. State supreme courts took steps to support renters and landlords alike: they crafted embargos on the stages of the eviction process controlled by courts, and many, via court order, also helped to facilitate the implementation of rent relief programs funded by local, state, and federal initiatives. Some of these high courts envisioned an even larger role for courts to play in staving off this wave of housing instability, with several supreme courts issuing orders that either mandated their trial courts participate in programs that kept people in their homes and out of court (i.e., eviction diversion programs) or authorized and encouraged individual courts within their systems to develop programs to accomplish these goals (Benfer et al. 2022).[1] This variation—in the ways courts approached diversion programs in particular—could serve as fertile ground for exploring the ways outside actors influence the administrative capacity of courts.

The implementation of statewide versus local court-based eviction diversion programs could be influenced by the level of support for such programs among different branches of government. External policy choices supportive of eviction diversion may be especially significant in states with administratively decentralized court systems, as these state supreme courts have limited capacity to control the procedural decisions of lower courts. For example, in Michigan and Texas, funding and collaboration between branches of government may have facilitated the establishment of statewide, court-based eviction diversion programs. In Michigan, funding allocated via a state legislative appropriation of federal funds, alongside an executive order by the state's governor establishing an eviction diversion program, contributed to the development of a statewide, court-based eviction diversion initiative.[2] In Texas, federal funds routed to the courts by the governor's office and inter-branch collaboration between executive agencies and the court system were noted in press releases regarding the rollout of Texas's program.[3]

In both states, the supreme court issued orders detailing how lower courts were to engage with the programs. In Michigan, participation in the program required lower courts to pause eviction proceedings for a period to allow for settlement negotiation outside of the formal court system.[4] In Texas, the supreme court mandated changes to eviction initiation forms to acknowledge the existence of the program.[5] These initiatives may demonstrate that inter-branch support through funding, executive orders, and collaboration can lead to the development of statewide court-based eviction diversion programs, even in states where the high courts have limited control over lower courts' procedural choices.

Inter-branch collaboration might have been key for supreme courts of states with decentralized court systems to have the necessary power to implement uniform procedural changes in response to the eviction crisis. The lack of such collaboration could explain why supreme courts in other administratively decentralized systems were unable to mandate statewide procedural changes. For example, the Illinois Supreme Court, which works within a relatively decentralized administrative system, permitted and encouraged trial courts to establish eviction diversion programs through a state supreme court order.[6] The Court's ability to create a statewide eviction diversion program that leveraged procedural changes may have been hindered by to the lack of inter-branch collaboration and extrajudicial policy change similar to that in Michigan and Texas. Without an external shift in its administrative role through externally supported policy change and resource allocation, the Illinois Supreme Court would not have the power to implement such changes.

The ability of supreme courts to implement procedural changes may vary based on the types of policy activities undertaken by other branches or their level of collaboration with external partners. Without such support, supreme courts—particularly in systems where they have limited control over court operational choices and case processing—may encounter difficulties in implementing widely applicable procedural changes. Future research could explore the impact of inter-branch collaboration or policy changes on procedural innovation, not only in the context of eviction diversion but also in other policy areas where court processes are implicated.

STAKEHOLDER ENGAGEMENT IN THE DEVELOPMENT OF COURT OPERATIONS POLICIES

The degree of centralization of administrative authority is undoubtedly a critical factor for understanding the features of policies that state supreme courts develop and lower courts' approaches to carrying them out. However, when state supreme courts seek to modify established rules and procedures through temporary and standard policymaking processes, they typically consult external sources for advice and recommendations, as demonstrated in chapters 3 and 4 (see also Clopton 2018). During the pandemic, court systems were forced to reevaluate existing policies, and the short-term policies implemented during this period had a significant impact on many stakeholder groups, including court staff, lower court judges, public and private attorneys, and parties to cases themselves. Consequently, the diversity of perspectives available for state supreme courts to consult during the policy revision process has likely expanded.

Chapter 3 offered evidence that gathering feedback and recommendations from implementers and other stakeholder groups during the pandemic was likely critical in securing their support of policy decisions, regardless of the extent to which a supreme court's concentration of administrative authority limited the decision-making power of lower court actors. Chapter 4 shed light on the formal advisory processes in state court procedure-making post-pandemic and also discussed some of the alternative information-seeking behaviors that supreme courts engage in. This section proposes an examination of the variation in how state supreme courts took advantage of the opportunity to engage with these additional perspectives, which may provide insights into the impact of such engagement—or lack thereof—on the legitimacy of the processes and the level of support for resulting policies.

Scholars studying policymaking emphasize the importance of involving a diverse array of stakeholders to increase long-term support for policies. Policymakers can enhance legitimacy by integrating stakeholder input at various stages using different methods. As examples, localized experimentation can generate new ideas and insights, even when policymakers prefer centralized decision-making (Schick 2002; Thatcher 2005; Saam and Kerber 2013). Despite policymakers' preference to retain control, they can engage a range of stakeholder audiences through formal channels to solicit feedback and improve buy-in and adherence to policy choices (Hooghe and Marks 2009; Thatcher 2002). Similarly, in the civil procedure-making literature, scholars explore the methods and benefits of seeking external viewpoints (Clopton 2018; Main 2014; see also Burbank and Farhang 2014, 2017). Standing advisory committees are a common method of obtaining external information, but questions have been raised about their effectiveness and lack of diversity (Clopton 2018, 40–41; Coleman 2018; see generally Ladha and Miller 1996; Epstein, Knight, and Martin 2003, 942–954).

A review of the key study states in this book reveals that supreme courts in more and less administratively centralized states may have taken different approaches to engaging new groups of external stakeholders in the making of case processing and operations policies. One set of states formed groups that were mandated to develop reports and materials that would provide guidance on best practices for court operations in the post-pandemic period, utilizing existing operational frameworks as a foundation for their recommendations. These groups were principally formed to assist supreme courts in developing plans for their systems' returns to full or in-person operations while adhering to public health and safety requirements. For example, the Kentucky Supreme Court established a series of task forces to assist its trial courts with phasing back into in-person proceedings and court business.[7] These groups sought feedback from stakeholders within their jurisdictions and offered suggestions to the Supreme Court based on their findings. Similarly, the Hawai`i Supreme Court formed the Committee on Operational Solutions and the Indiana Supreme Court formed the Resuming Court Operations Task Force, both of which were tasked with examining their respective system's capacity to conduct remote matters, developing plans for a safe return to normal operations.[8]

In both centralized and decentralized state court systems, supreme courts have established groups to develop best practices within their existing operational frameworks. However, in more administratively decentralized states, high courts may have also assigned these groups a more expansive set of responsibilities, directing them to identify rules and processes that could be permanently modified to incorporate technology. This could be due to the fact that in a more decentralized system, these supreme courts may be conscious of the fact that obtaining buy-in from lower court actors and other stakeholder groups may be critical to ensuring the sustainability of any policy changes made post-pandemic (e.g., Ansell, Sørensen, and Torfing 2021; see also Ansell and Gash 2008; Emerson and Nabatchi 2015). While groups formed by supreme courts in more administratively centralized systems may have provided recommendations with the goal of "spur[ring] further conversation and action" regarding revisions to bodies of generally applicable policies, groups in states where lower courts had more freedom to address pandemic response locally were often explicitly assigned this responsibility.[9]

For example, the supreme courts of Nevada and Ohio created groups to identify rules and processes in existing generally applicable bodies of regulations relevant to remote proceedings and remote court services that they would suggest revising. Supreme courts in decentralized states also offered other forms of broad mandates to the groups they formed. As another example, the Florida Supreme Court's Workgroup on the Continuity of Court Operations and Proceedings During and After COVID-19 was authorized not only to identify changes that needed to be made to existing court rules and procedures but also to make appeals to the legislature to change statute if they deemed it necessary. In some decentralized states, groups' purposes evolved over time, with some starting with a narrower focus and expanding to that of proposing new rules and modifications to existing rules. For example, in the case of Texas, the Supreme Court initially established the Remote Proceedings Task Force as a body to gather information about extant rules and procedures, tasking it with developing a report identifying the "barriers to continuing remote online proceedings and court innovations developed as a result of the COVID-19 pandemic."[10] After the task force submitted its report to the Court, the chief justice of Texas increased the group's scope of work, drafting a memo empowering the task force to "[draft] rule amendments to remove impediments to and support the use of remote proceedings."[11]

Stakeholder groups formed by courts may have influenced proposals for policy changes in ways that may not have been anticipated given the level of administrative centralization within a court system and its supreme court's approach to policymaking during the pandemic. For instance, the Vermont Supreme Court, which heads a relatively centralized court system, is considering a change to its civil procedural rule on hearing participation methods that would delegate significant authority to lower courts. This move is surprising given the Court's more tightly controlled approach to pandemic response, but it may be attributed to the responsibilities assigned to its Special Advisory Committee on Remote Hearings. This committee was specifically charged with proposing changes to court rules related to remote participation. One proposal it has advanced for consideration would permit judges to establish locally applicable lists of presumptively remote and in-person hearing types through standing orders, granting lower court judges considerable authority in determining standard appearance modalities across cases. This proposal is distinct from other lists of presumptively remote and in-person case types that have been codified into generally applicable bodies of rules, like that in Michigan described in chapter 4, and would empower lower court judges to make these choices. Although we cannot say what rules would be under consideration in Vermont without this committee and its specific mandate from the Court, the work of this committee and others highlights the value of exploring the role they played in post-pandemic rulemaking processes.

Some of these groups have been tasked with developing reports on best practices, while others have been specifically directed to propose policy changes to their respective supreme courts. Among the groups in the latter category, certain groups have suggested policies that align with what would be expected given a court system's approach to making temporary policies during the pandemic and its level of administrative centralization. However, there are others that have advanced somewhat unexpected suggestions from a theoretical perspective. Regardless of their individual approaches to engaging with advisory bodies, supreme courts generally exhibit a willingness to seek out information to aid in developing their post-pandemic policy strategies. This engagement took many forms and could yield concrete advantages, such as recommendations that lead to proposed or adopted policy changes, as well as potential longer-term benefits related to how court actors perceive the legitimacy of decision-making processes and outcomes given their involvement. The impacts of collaborating with these groups, and the integration of their contributions into decision-making processes and policy outputs, warrant further study.

Exploring Avenues for Future Research on Technology-Driven Procedural Change

The conclusion of chapter 2 briefly touched on additional ways that administrative policy tools could be aggregated to study how supreme courts craft other types of case processing and court operations policies. In that chapter, I suggested that the assignment of control over court-annexed methods of alternative dispute resolution (ADR) — to state-level actors, local-level actors, or to both in a shared system of power — could help explain why state court systems design different systems of rules regarding the use of ADR. For ADR in particular, the remote-relevant administrative centralization score from chapter 2 could also be a useful indicator for explaining differences in ADR policies. Scholars could apply either measure to a study of the temporary ADR-related policies developed by state court systems in response to the pandemic, or to those permanent forms of policy that are more durable outside of the pandemic context.

Courts' approaches to designing temporary policies for court-annexed ADR during the pandemic may have varied depending on who holds the practical power to manage ADR programs as well as on the degree of technology-relevant administrative centralization in a state. For instance, in Michigan and Florida, state-level court administrators share responsibilities over court-annexed ADR with lower courts and are relatively more administratively decentralized on remote-relevant dimensions. The temporary policies regarding how ADR would proceed in these states were presented more as guidance than as mandates. In Michigan, the Supreme Court provided guidance documents encouraging courts to triage options available for resolving cases, suggesting they consider ADR when appropriate.[12] In Florida, the Supreme Court reported out an approved recommendation from the workgroup it formed, offering that ADR was a form of case resolution that was "amenable to being conducted remotely."[13] In both cases, the approaches reflect the states' more decentralized approaches to ADR administration. Individual judges and courts retain some autonomy over how they handle cases and whether to use ADR. This decentralized approach allows for flexibility and adaptability but may also result in inconsistent use of ADR across different courts or jurisdictions.

In contrast, in Vermont, state-level administrators reported having full control over the administration of court-annexed ADR in the NCSC SCO survey, as well as a high level of control over technology-relevant administrative policy tools. During the pandemic, the Vermont Supreme Court promulgated a temporary policy that authorized remote participation in mediation, a method of ADR, without a stipulation or further court order, pursuant to the state's civil procedural rules for the duration of the judicial emergency.[14] Vermont's policy is reflective of the state's centralized approach to ADR and its management of technology-relevant administrative policy tools, enabling the promulgation of a policy that promotes greater uniformity and consistency across the state's courts.

There are a number of other areas of operational policies that scholars could explore to expand the application of the remote-relevant administrative centralization scale. Another contrast between Florida's approach to the construction of pandemic policy related to electronic evidence and Vermont's is instructive. The Florida Supreme Court endorsed a set of best practices proposed by a pandemic policy workgroup for managing electronic evidence, whereas Vermont's Rules for Electronic Filing specify formatting guidelines for exhibits submitted via the state's e-filing system.[15] These contrasting approaches, one focused on best practices and the other on specific requirements, may further underscore the differing degrees of control that each state has over the management of remote technologies. It would be valuable to investigate the diverse approaches of state court systems in crafting ADR and evidence management policies, particularly by examining the temporary policies enacted during the pandemic, as well as those proposed and adopted changes in states' permanent policies in the post-pandemic period.

Additionally, work could be done to track permanent policy changes across the areas examined in chapter 4. For example, that chapter acknowledged that changes to the Vermont Rules of Civil Procedure, which provide for standardization of processes for nonevidentiary and evidentiary hearings—as well as for remote and hybrid hearings, among other remote-relevant process changes—were pending at the time of writing.[16] Massachusetts also sought comments on a proposed change to signature requirements for court documents, proposing to permit pleadings in civil cases to be signed electronically, with comments due by early 2024.[17] Tracking the development of these final policy solutions' adoption will provide further testing of the ways in which state court systems translate features of their temporary policy environment to states' rules of civil procedure and other generally applicable bodies of law.

The findings in chapter 2 also suggest the need for further research to explore the relationship between the control of specific administrative tools at the local or central level and the policy language chosen by supreme courts, particularly in states where control over these tools is more evenly distributed across the court system. Arizona, where state- and lower court-level actors share information technology responsibilities, is a case in point. In response to the pandemic, the Arizona Supreme Court delegated authority to lower courts to determine the use of communication technologies for remote hearings and encouraged the use of online dispute resolution platforms.[18] These actions could shed light on how the distribution of power over information technology led the Supreme Court to provide authorizations and guidance instead of imposing stricter requirements or specifying the types of cases that could be heard remotely. In

Georgia, another state that falls in closer to the middle of the scale, state court administrators reported having no control over the management of lower court facilities. In its early guidance, the Georgia Supreme Court urged different classes of courts sharing courthouse facilities or operating in the same counties to coordinate their guidelines, suggesting that the Supreme Court's management of operational choices related to activities occurring within courthouses themselves would be limited.[19]

Collaborating with Courts to Build the Evidence Base

The proposed extensions to this project could be carried out by utilizing existing observational data, including information collected to support the empirical studies in this book and data that could be gathered from other publicly available sources. These sources include states' legislative materials (e.g., bill texts, hearing transcripts) and judicial resources (e.g., court operations task force meeting minutes, reports) posted on state government websites and in physical repositories. While these suggested studies have great potential to enrich our understanding of administrative power in court systems, there are likely additional opportunities to engage in theory building and empirical research that necessitate an expansion of the evidence base (see generally Pew Charitable Trusts 2023c; Carpenter et al. 2022a; Sandefur 2016; see also Alexander and Sudeall 2023). Scholars will face choices regarding whether these efforts should take a quantitative or qualitative direction. In either case, shifting our focus beyond the formal arrangements of administrative authority within court systems also reveals the need for novel data to address emerging questions in this area of research.

As an example, this project's findings highlight the fact that existing sources of information used to describe the organizational features of court systems may inadequately capture the complete range of informal behaviors and uses of administrative power by lower court actors. To achieve a more nuanced understanding of how this form of authority operates in state court systems, it becomes necessary to explore alternative methods of capturing and explaining these informal practices across jurisdictions.

One possible approach could involve leveraging an interview method, such as the one employed in chapter 3, to systematically collect information on these practices both across and within states. To successfully conduct a study of this magnitude, scholars would need to devise strategies for collaborating with courts, ensuring that they can gather the necessary data while also safeguarding the privacy of their informants (see, e.g., Pew Charitable Trusts 2023a, 2023c). Those working in lower courts in particular may encounter difficulties in openly discussing their informal practices due to concerns about disclosing behaviors that could be perceived as noncompliant with directives from higher courts. Creating a supportive setting that encourages lower court actors to share their experiences and practices candidly is critical to gaining a comprehensive understanding of the use of administrative power within court systems.

Besides the researchers whose work would be enriched through the development of a more nuanced measure of administrative power in state court systems, courts themselves would also benefit from a more thorough accounting of how this power operates in their systems. But given the concerns surrounding self-reporting noncompliant behavior, it may be difficult for court systems to accurately account for the distribution of administrative authority in their systems through self-study. Thus, it may be useful for courts to partner with independent researchers who have relevant substantive and methodological expertise.

Crisis and Calm: Actionable Strategies for Courts, Civil Justice Advocates, and Their Research Partners

The current project holds significance not only for a range of scholarly conversations but also for court actors and civil justice advocates who may seek to incorporate the findings into their work and institutional practices. Principally, while the focus of this book is describing the dynamics of procedural change during the COVID-19 pandemic, its aim was to use this disruptive event as a vehicle for studying the mechanisms that govern procedural change and implementation more generally. Approaching the book's contributions from this perspective permits us to extend the relevance of its findings both to emergency situations and to the everyday experiences of courts and their users.

Inter- and Intra-branch Dynamics: Anticipating Roadblocks to Procedural Reform

First, if we consider the relevance of the findings for our understanding of courts' responses to emergencies, the lessons learned from the COVID-19 pandemic can inform courts' continuity of operations planning for other emergency situations. While some courts had previously included components in their plans to address pandemics and public health emergencies, many did not, leaving them less prepared for the unique challenges posed by the pandemic. In the post-pandemic period, it will be important for courts to reconsider their continuity of operations plans to account for such emergencies, while also acknowledging the importance of both formal and informal exercises of administrative power within their court systems. By taking a more comprehensive approach to understanding the distribution of administrative power within the court system, courts can be better prepared to respond promptly and flexibly to unique situations, whether at the state or local level.

A more nuanced understanding of the distribution of administrative power within a court system can have important implications for a system's internal operations. Specifically, gaining such an understanding may facilitate courts' reflections on how their systems respond to change, helping courts to anticipate potential roadblocks in procedural reform projects. The findings of this project reveal that one critical factor in the successful implementation of procedural changes is the extent to which lower court actors perceive their level of administrative independence. By understanding these intra-branch administrative power dynamics, court systems can better incorporate lower courts' input into decision-making around procedural and operational changes or use alternative tactics to prevent implementation problems.

Understanding the administrative power landscape in a given state court system can also help facilitate productive inter-branch relations in times of both crisis and calm. Understanding how court systems are structured administratively is a complex endeavor, and it is not unreasonable to assume that bodies such as legislatures, which hold the authority to make policies and appropriations relevant to a court system's activities, have a limited understanding of their administrative organization. In both routine communications and in coordinating emergency requests, clear communication by courts about their structures may avert conflicts with policymakers and appropriations bodies. Misunderstandings concerning the degree of centralization within a court system may result in misallocated funding or policies crafted with language that impedes successful implementation efforts on the part of courts. Better communication of court organization to external bodies may thus result in more constructive relationships between courts and policymakers, enhancing the efficacy of external policy choices that affect court procedures.

Procedural Design and the Court User Experience

The aim of this project was to provide scholars, court professionals, and advocates for civil justice reform alike with insights about courts' internal operations and administrative decision-making practices through the lens of the COVID-19 pandemic. But in addition to what the pandemic moment can teach us about administrative power, it has brought to light a previously underestimated capability of courts—their ability to be flexible in how they approach providing services to the public. Consequently, the pandemic also has provided an opportunity to reconsider how people interact with courts and their perceptions of those interactions.

Notably, the pandemic experience drew attention to the fact that, in many jurisdictions across the country, courts were not designed in ways that adequately met the needs of the people who used them. For the average, self-represented court user—who is representative of the vast majority of those who use civil courts—it was difficult to navigate the many steps and processes required to resolve a civil legal problem before the pandemic (Carpenter et al. 2022b; Shanahan et al. 2016, 2020; Rickard and Naqui 2021; Pew Charitable Trusts 2021; Buenger 2020; Spaulding 2020; Rickard 2017). Many of the procedural changes that were made in response to the circumstances created by the pandemic have likely made courts easier for this group to use (Zarnow and Hirsch 2021). Examples throughout the book have acknowledged the consequences of procedural change for court users. For example, modifications to notarization requirements for self-represented people—a change made by courts in some jurisdictions and by legislative or gubernatorial action in others—removed a step in the document filing process, making it easier for these litigants to submit documents to courts. As another example, changes to court rules to permit remote participation in hearings reduced the monetary and temporal costs associated with arranging to attend a court hearing in person, leading to a reduction in default hearings and an increase in party and witness participation more broadly in studied jurisdictions (see, e.g., JTC 2020; Quintanilla et al. 2023b; Hoffman and Strezhnev 2023).

Along with bringing about the types of procedural changes that likely increased access to the courts, the widespread mandate for a response to the pandemic permitted us to observe the unequal distribution of these innovations across jurisdictions. For example, in the case of eviction diversion programs as described earlier in this chapter, we observed that some states implemented universally applicable eviction diversion initiatives, whereas in other states the discretionary nature of the programs led to patchworks of implementation within a single state. In other states such programs were never introduced as part of their COVID-19 harm reduction plans (Benfer et al, 2022).

While these changes to court processes are just a small

sample of the range of procedural modifications courts implemented, they demonstrate how institutional change can alter people's experiences with courts in disparate ways: in some jurisdictions, forms may be easier to file, it may be less costly to attend a hearing, a program may be offered that leads to a fruitful negotiation between a landlord and a tenant. The choice over implementing these reforms (or not) and permanently codifying them (or not) motivates important questions about the differences in the experiences and outcomes of people using civil courts according to the procedural regime of their jurisdictions, both as it pertains to cross-sectional questions (i.e., differences across jurisdictions) and temporal questions (i.e., "old" and "new" institutional forms within jurisdictions).

Scholars are conducting work to better understand people's experiences with new processes, within and across jurisdictions, as it relates to their perceptions of fairness, trust in judicial institutions, and the judgments they obtain in cases. For example, a host of studies have focused on people's experiences with remote and hybrid hearings during the pandemic, finding that parties feel more engaged (e.g., Mulcahy, Rowden, and Teeder 2020; Mulcahy, Rowden, and Tsalapatanis 2022; but see Rossner and Tait 2023), view proceedings as more procedurally fair, and have higher rates of satisfaction with case outcomes (e.g., Quintanilla et al. 2023b). Evidence also suggests that when parties have the option to appear in court remotely, rates of default decrease (e.g., Hoffman and Strezhnev 2023; see also JTC 2020; National Center for State Courts 2023). Of course, employing technologies to facilitate court hearings is not a novel development arising out of the pandemic. A substantial body of scholarly work has extolled the virtues of technology-mediated hearings while also offering cautionary notes about the differences in case processing when compared to the "gold standard" of in-person hearings as well as concerns regarding the digital divide (for a review see, e.g., Bannon and Adelstein 2020; Bulinski and Prescott 2015; Sternlight and Robbennolt 2022).

Researchers, advocacy groups, and courts have also developed best practices guides and reports that have advanced access to justice arguments for making the changes observed during the pandemic more durable and widespread.[20] These resources aim to sustain programs like eviction diversion initiatives (Nazem 2022; see also Gold, Guerin, and Lowrey 2022; Benfer et al. 2021), outline best practices for making pandemic-era procedural modifications like remote and hybrid hearings rules durable (Spulak 2024; see also Bannon and Keith 2020; Thumma and Reinkensmeyer 2022), and establish frameworks for simplifying court processes (National Center for State Courts Access to Justice 2023; Pew Charitable Trusts 2023b). Membership organizations representing state court administrators and chief justices have also advanced sets of principles (e.g., CCJ/COSCA 2020) and resolutions (e.g., CCJ/COSCA 2021) in support of such initiatives.

In sum, this moment was a pivotal one for courts, offering them opportunities to reconsider their operational practices, assess the loci of decision-making regarding those practices, and reflect on how these elements of court administration affect the people these institutions serve. The pandemic underscored the fact that there must be a consideration of the actual users of these institutions when making choices about how they are designed. Moving forward, it will be imperative for courts to retain a degree of flexibility and responsiveness to the needs of their users in their choices over procedural design. Courts should also actively promote and welcome scrutiny and examination of their work, sharing data with interested scholars (see, e.g., Pew Charitable Trusts 2023a, 2023c). It is essential that we understand how different administrative power structures—and the complex dynamics they create—affect the ability of courts to create and put into practice new rules and procedures. These commitments will play a pivotal role in achieving broad access to these institutions, sparing us from having to wait for the next crisis to trigger another wave of transformative change.

Notes

Introduction

1. For example, Alaska employed a liberal approach to remote appearances in criminal matters before the pandemic. Individuals could appear remotely for minor offenses, like misdemeanors and traffic citations, as well as when defendants would have to travel a significant distance in order to reach a courthouse (Alaska R RCRP 5.1(e)(1)(A), Alaska R RCRP Rule 6(3)(B), in John Greacen, "Remote Appearances of Parties, Attorneys, and Witnesses: A Review of Current Court Rules and Practices," *Self-Represented Litigation Network* (8) 2017.

2. National Center for State Courts, "Case Studies in ODR for Courts," 2020, https://www.ncsc.org/__data/assets/pdf_file/0020/16517/2020-01-28-odr-case-studies-v2-final.pdf.

3. E.g., Kentucky Supreme Court, "Updates on COVID-19 and Court Operations," March 17, 2020. See also Kentucky Supreme Court, "COVID-19 and the Courts: An Update from Chief Justice Minton," March 26, 2020; Massachusetts Supreme Judicial Court, "Order Limiting In-Person Appearances in State Courthouses to Emergency Matters That Cannot Be Resolved through a Videoconference or Telephonic Hearing," March 17, 2020.

4. E.g., 28th Judicial District of Kentucky, "Administrative Order for Proceedings during Kentucky Court of Justice COVID-19 Emergency Response," May 27, 2020; 37th Judicial Circuit of Kentucky, "In Re: Civil Motion Hour for June 1, 2020," May 26, 2020; 55th Judicial Circuit of Kentucky, "General Order Supplementing Kentucky Supreme Court Orders 2020–39/40 in Response to the COVID-19 Emergency," May 28. 2020.

5. E.g., District Court of Massachusetts, "District Court Standing Order 3-20 Court Operations under the Exigent Circumstances Created by COVID-19 (coronavirus)," April 6, 2020; Suffolk County Superior Court, "Suffolk Civil County—Guidelines for Operation for Civil Session during COVID-19 Pandemic," March 31, 2020; Middlesex County Superior Court, "Middlesex County—Guidelines for Operation for Civil Session during COVID-19 Pandemic," April 3, 2020.

6. E.g., Massachusetts Supreme Judicial Court, "Order Regarding Court Operations under the Exigent Circumstances Created by the COVID-19 (Coronavirus) Pandemic," April 1, 2020. See also Kentucky Supreme Court,

"In Re: Kentucky Court of Justice Response to COVID-19 Emergency," April 1, 2020; Massachusetts Superior Court, "Updated Protocol Governing Superior Court Operations during the Coronavirus (COVID-19) Pandemic," April 29, 2020; Commonwealth of Kentucky Barren District and Circuit Courts, Divisions I and II, "General Order," May 27, 2020.

7. E.g., District Court of Massachusetts, "District Court Standing Order 3–20 Court Operations under the Exigent Circumstances Created by COVID-19 (Coronavirus)," April 6, 2020.

8. 20th Judicial Circuit of Florida, "In Re: Mitigating Measures in Response to COVID-19," May 11, 2020 ("when"); 13th Judicial Circuit of Florida, "Court Proceedings during COVID-19 Mitigation Efforts—Phase II," April 15, 2020 ("if"); 17th Judicial Circuit of Florida, "Third Emergency Administrative Order: Coronavirus Disease 2019 (COVID-19)," April 6, 2020 ("wherever").

9. 15th Judicial Circuit of Florida, "In Re: Mitigating Measures in Response to COVID-19," April 17, 2020.

10. 16th Judicial Circuit Court of Missouri, "In Re: Court Operations during COVID-19 Stay at Home/Shelter in Place Order," March 22, 2020. See also 17th Judicial Circuit Court of Missouri, "Administrative Order 2020–0322," March 24, 2020.

11. 22nd Judicial Circuit of Missouri, "In Re: COVID-19 Order 13," March 24, 2020. See also 10th Judicial Circuit of Missouri, "In Re Court Operations in Light of the Missouri Governor's Order of March 21, 2020 and the Orders of the Supreme Court Dated March 22, 2020, April 1, 2020, and April 17, 2020," April 20, 2020.

12. 34th Judicial Circuit Court of Missouri, "In Re: COVID-19–In Person Proceedings and Social Distancing in Courtrooms, Circuit Clerk's Offices, Juvenile Offices and Other Court Offices," March 30, 2020.

13. 14th Judicial Circuit of Missouri, "In Re: COVID-19," March 16, 2020.

14. This number represents states that report caseload statistics to the National Center for State Courts (NCSC) Court Statistics Project. In a typical year, more than 90 percent of states provide these data, but these data are still both imperfectly categorized and are likely incomplete, even in reporting states (see Shanahan et al. 2022 for comprehensive reporting of these data).

15. E.g., Legal Services Corporation, "The Justice Gap: The Unmet Legal Needs of Low-Income Americans," 2022; Utah Bar Foundation, "The Justice Gap: Addressing the Unmet Legal Needs of Lower-Income Utahns," 2020.

16. See, e.g., the NCSC's "Nebraska Self-Represented Litigants Report" (2021, 19) which maps the steps a self-represented litigant must take in order to get divorced and the opportunities for a party to fail to navigate procedure therein (https://bit.ly/3rVdmyG).

17. Charles Kindregan and Patricia Kindregan, "Pro Se Litigants: The Challenge of the Future," Probate and Family Court Department, Massachusetts Courts Pro Se Committee Report, 1995, quoted in Jessica K. Steinberg, "Demand Side Reform in the Poor People's Court," *Connecticut Law Review* 47 (2014): 741–805.

18. In terms of convenience, many studies now suggest that permitting remote appearances at hearings has significantly decreased default judgments in high-volume dockets such as eviction. For example, see Thumma and Reinkensmeyer (2022, 19) for a discussion of increased appearance rates in the context of landlord tenant hearings.

19. In terms of accessibility, remote hearing guides have advocated for virtual hearing rooms to be equipped with "closed captioning, keyboard accessibility, automatic transcripts, and screen reader support, as a minimum" (4), all of which offer a more inclusive courtroom experience for those with disabilities. See California Commission on Access to Justice, adapted by the Conference of Chief Justices and Conference of State Court Administrators, "Remote Hearings and Access to Justice during COVID-19 and Beyond," https://www.ncsc.org/__data/assets/pdf _file/0018/40365/RRT-Technology-ATJ-Remote-Hearings-Guide.pdf, accessed August 1, 2022.

20. I note that there are other fields and scholarly traditions that contribute to the research on decision-making among judicial professionals. However, this project will focus on analyzing the differences between these two specific bodies of literature and the theoretical frameworks that underpin them.

Chapter 1. Navigating Administrative Power in State Court Systems

1. Another possibility is that lower courts aren't fearful per se of monitoring via appeals, but that instead judges are motivated to find the "right answer" and thus the appeals process is meant to serve more as an error correction method than a way to punish shirking or rein in deviant preferences (Kornhauser 1995; Shavell 1995).

2. For a survey of how state supreme courts acknowledge their general administrative authority, see Mark 2024.

3. NCSL, "Speedy Trial Rights," https://www.ncsl.org/research/civil -and-criminal-justice/speedy-trial-rights.aspx, accessed August 1, 2022; see also NACDL, "Court Backlogs & Speedy Trial," https://www.nacdl.org /Content/Court-Backlogs-Speedy-Trial, accessed August 1, 2022.

4. NCSL, "Speedy Trial Rights," e.g., 725 ILCS 5/103-5(a-b), Tenn. Code S. 40-38-116, Utah Code S 77-1-6(f).

5. "The Delaware Supreme Court has, however, issued an administrative directive calling on Superior Court to adjudicate 90% of criminal cases

within 120 days of indictment and 100% within one year. That administrative directive, however, creates no rights independent of the [general] constitutional right to a speedy trial." DE Supreme Court Administrative Directive No. 130 (July 11, 2001) cited in *Delaware v. Duonnolo* 2020, 3. See also *Delaware v. Lacy* 2021, 4.

6. The courts have prioritized some civil matters such as hearings for temporary civil protection from domestic violence, emergency guardianship matters, and mental health or substance abuse commitment hearings with the aim of protecting public safety.

7. Supreme Court of Illinois, "In re: Illinois Courts Response to COVID-19 Emergency," April 7, 2020.

8. Annie Knox, "Halt to Jury Trials Frustrates Victims, but Program Allowing Their Return Sparks Safety Questions," *Deseret News*, February 6, 2021, https://www.deseret.com/utah/2021/2/6/22254755/halt-to-jury-trials-frustrates-victims-but-pilot-program-allowing-return-coronavirus-jer rod-baum.

9. Work on the proliferation of varying sets of federal district court rules highlights decreased uniformity in the application of the federal rules at the federal level. It is hypothesized that this rule diffusion has also inspired "procedural experimentation" at the state level. In the case of discovery rules discussed by Moskowitz (2002, quoted in Koppel 2005), states have endeavored to pilot a variety of procedural modifications in an effort to make "civil litigation cheaper, faster, and more efficient" (p. 599). Furthermore, while the virtues of procedural uniformity are certainly baked into the idea of a body of statutory or rule-based procedure (e.g., Main 2001), recent scholarship debates the value and applicability of standardized procedure to the modern state civil court (e.g., Bookman and Shanahan 2022; see also a historical account by Subrin and Main 2016).

10. These states are also referred to as "code" procedure states. See Clopton (2018) for a comprehensive analysis. For an alternative analysis, see Reinhart and Coppolo (2002).

11. E.g., in the state of Florida, where the legislature can repeal a court-promulgated rules change by a two-thirds majority vote, such repeals are rare events; see footnotes 29–31 in CS/HUR 7111 Final Bill Analysis, 2011, https://flsenate.gov/Session/Bill/2011/7111/Analyses/h7111z.JDC .PDF.

12. There are exceptions. For example, while landlord/tenant matters may rely on civil procedural rules, these rules may be modified for such dockets, which may also use different sets of forms and rely on different time thresholds for procedural steps; see, e.g., a reference to the differentiation of landlord/tenant and small claims matters in the D.C. courts' civil procedural rules, https://www.dccourts.gov/sites/default /files/2017-11/Superior%20Court%20Rules%20of%20Civil%20Procedure.pdf.

13. There is debate on this point given the ideological, demographic, and socioeconomic imbalance in who gets a say in constructing procedure. Coleman (2018) provides a helpful overview of the historical demographic homogeneity of the federal rulemaking body. See also Burbank and Farhang 2017; Stempel 2001; and Mullenix 1991.

14. E.g., "Cases Not Given Priority. Within the list of cases that are not given priority, judges, magistrates, and staff should exercise their judgment and give primacy based on the facts and circumstances of each case: Foreclosure actions, Civil actions for recovery of money damages, Small claims, Administrative appeals under chapter 17A, Probate other than guardianships, Other law and equity cases," Iowa Supreme Court, July 9, 2020; "Low priority cases, such as final hearings on divorces without children, proceedings supplemental, civil jury trials, and estate matters may be delayed, conducted remotely," Indiana Supreme Court re: Owen Circuit Courts, June 9, 2020. On file with author.

15. Rule 83, Rules by District Courts; Judge's Directives, "(a) Local Rules," 2007.

16. Utah Code of Judicial Administration, 2-204, "Local Supplemental Rules," 2023.

17. Rules of Supreme Court of Virginia, 1:15, "Local Rules of Court," 2021.

18. Indiana Rules of Court, Rules of Trial Procedure, Rule 81, "Local Court Rules," 2023.

19. Uniform Superior Court Rules, State of Georgia Council of Superior Court Judges, Rule 1.2, "Authority to Enact Rules Which Deviate from the Uniform Superior Court Rules," 2017.

20. Uniform Superior Court Rules, State of Georgia Council of Superior Court Judges, Rule 1.2, 2017.

21. 735 ILCS 5/1-104 (b) (from Ch. 110, par. 1-104).

22. Arkansas Supreme Court, "In re Changes to Arkansas Rules of Civil Proc., 294 Ark. Appx. 664" (1987).

23. It should be noted that there is an alternative interpretation of these callouts. Perhaps they grant local courts the same power to establish local rules as permissive states, as determinations of "housekeeping" matters might be quite broad in interpretation.

24. See Friedman and Chemerinsky (1995) for a proposal that offers lower courts (in the federal system) opportunities to experiment with local rules while being subject to similar monitoring mechanisms.

25. See also the National Center for State Courts' Library eCollection for an array of useful resources related to both state- and interstate-level court operations guides,https://ncsc.contentdm.oclc.org/digital/collection/ctadmin, accessed January 3, 2022.

26. For an overview of the various approaches to measuring centralization, see Raftery (2015).

27. For an alternative approach to measuring these features of administrative power, see Henderson (1984).

28. While the survey has been administered since 2016, it no longer includes this battery of questions.

29. Judicial appointments are not discussed in the following explanation since this power is not exclusively within the purview of the judiciary, but rather, it can be a shared responsibility with the legislative and/or executive branches of government.

30. States that did not respond are Idaho, Maine, Montana, Nebraska, New York, Oklahoma, Virginia, and Wyoming.

Chapter 2. Linking Administrative Capacity and State Supreme Courts' Policy Choices during the Pandemic

1. The CDC has the authority to make certain regulations, but there are limitations on the specific things it can regulate. With that said, it might not always be clear if the CDC has the authority to address a particular issue. For example, the CDC had issued a mandate requiring people to wear masks on airplanes and forms of public transportation that a judge later ruled the CDC did not have the authority to issue (*Health Freedom Defense Fund et al. v. Biden* 2022). Agency interpretations of their own authority are not often successfully challenged in court, but they are increasingly so. There is an ongoing debate among scholars about how much deference should be given to agencies as they tackle novel and complex policy issues; see generally Lisa Bressman and Kevin Stack, "Chevron Is a Phoenix," *Vanderbilt Law Review* 74 (2021): 465–482.

2. For a treatment that applies this logic to the field of platform governance, or the rules and regulations that determine how online platforms use user data, moderate content, and engage with users, see Sean Martin McDonald, "The Fiduciary Supply Chain," Centre for International Governance Innovation, October 28, 2019, www.cigionline.org/articles/fiduciary-supply-chain/.

3. For an alternative treatment, see Joshua Hernandez, "A Survey of Civil Procedure: Technology to COVID-19 within State Courts," *Marquette Law Review* 105, 4 (2022): 963–1004.

4. E.g., after listing a number of emergency and essential services, the Iowa Supreme Court states in its April 2, 2020 order that "this list is not intended to be exclusive and judicial officers shall determine what constitutes an emergency within the meaning of this paragraph." On file with author. As another example, while the Indiana Supreme Court directed lower courts to attend to "only [the] most critical hearings," it permitted judges to "use their discretion in determining which cases [would] be heard." June 9, 2020. On file with author.

5. For more information about procurement policies and concerns over possible mismatches between courts' processes and the acquisition of technology, see Jason Tashea, "A Human Rights Approach to Justice Technology Procurement," *Georgetown Law Technology Review*, online, September 2023; and Access to Justice Team, *Contracting Digital Services for Courts* (Williamsburg, VA: National Center for State Courts, 2022).

6. I categorize control over these tools as total (3), shared (2), or local (1) and created an additive scale by summing these indicators. The resulting scale has high internal consistency (alpha = .89).

7. "Re: Video-Conference Security Concerns," memorandum to the Alabama State Bar from Rich Hobson, Administrative Director of Courts, April 8, 2020.

8. Chief Justice of Kentucky, "Update for May 15, 2020."

9. Chief Justice of Kentucky, "Addressing Bumps in the Road as We Plan for Reopening Week 2," June 5, 2020.

10. E.g., Chief Justice of Michigan, "Regarding: Expanding Remote Proceedings," April 7, 2020; and Michigan Supreme Court Administrative Office, "Process for Triaging Case Actions during the COVID-19 Crisis," April 28, 2020; "Information Concerning Mail Opening Services," May 1, 2020; "Remote Court Participation Chart," May 11, 2020.

11. E.g., Supreme Court of Ohio, "Specialized Docket Certification Standards, COVID Guidance," April 23, 2020; Texas State Office of Court Administration, "Guidance for All Court Proceedings during the COVID-19 Pandemic (for Proceedings on or after June 1, 2020)," May 4, 2020; Supreme Court of Missouri, "Operational Directives," May 4, 2020.

12. Michigan Supreme Court, "Order Limiting Activities/Assemblages in Court Facilities," March 18, 2020; see also "Temporary Amendments and Extensions Related to Continuing Work in Courts," April 17, 2020. Both on file with author.

13. Since the early 2000s, many courts have engaged in some form of digital migration. Instead of processing physical documents submitted by lawyers and parties, some courts had already adopted relatively robust e-filing systems, while others had implemented systems limited to certain types of parties and cases. Before the pandemic, about three-quarters of the states (and the District of Columbia) could point to jurisdictions that allowed self-represented litigants to electronically file documents in some civil case types, and all had implemented systems where attorneys were either permitted or mandated to e-file. Even though the vast majority of courts had adopted some form of electronic document filing system before the pandemic, there was variance in the platforms used, the types of parties that were able to use them, and the case types that qualified for e-filing both within and between states. See Pew Charitable Trusts, "How Courts Embraced Technology, Met the Pandemic Challenge, and Revolutionized Their Operations," https://www.pewtrusts.org/-/media

/assets/2021/12/how-courts-embraced-technology.pdf. See also National Center for State Courts, "Self-Represented Efiling: Surveying the Accessible Implementations," 2022, https://www.ncsc.org/__data/assets/pdf _file/0022/76432/SRL-efiling-1.pdf.

14. To note, the Michigan courts are in the process of rolling out a statewide e-filing system, MI file, but it is currently very limited in its implementation in the trial courts (see https://info.courts.mi.gov/hubfs /mifilecourtlist.pdf for more information).

15. Chief Justice of Louisiana, untitled memo to Louisiana Courts, April 21, 2020; Michigan Supreme Court, "In re Emergency Procedures in Court Facilities, Administrative Order No. 2020-1," March 15, 2020.

16. Supreme Court of Tennessee, "Order Suspending In-Person Court Proceedings," March 13, 2020.

17. Supreme Court of Missouri, "In re: Operational Directives for Easing COVID-19 Restrictions on In-Person Proceedings," May 4, 2020.

18. Supreme Court of Texas, "Twelfth Emergency Order regarding the COVID-19 State of Disaster," April 27, 2020; Michigan Supreme Court, "Order Expanding Authority for Judicial Officers to Conduct Proceedings Remotely, Administrative Order No. 2020-6," April 7, 2020.

19. Specific reference to Supreme Court of Tennessee, "Order Suspending In-Person Court Proceedings," March 13, 2020, but this language appears across orders, including those promulgated on March 25, April 24, and May 26, 2020.

20. Commonwealth of Massachusetts Supreme Judicial Court, "Second Updated Order regarding Court Operations under the Exigent Circumstances Created by the COVID-19 (Coronavirus) Pandemic," May 26, 2020.

21. Vermont Supreme Court, "Administration Order 49: Declaration of Judicial Emergency and Changes to Court Procedures and Miscellaneous Information," March 17, 2020.

22. Connecticut Supreme Court, "Simplifying the Process for Self-Represented Parties to E-file Their Documents," May 11, 2020.

23. Supreme Court of Tennessee, "Order Extending State of Emergency and Easing Suspension of In-Person Court Proceedings," May 26, 2020.

24. Supreme Court of Florida, "In re: COVID-19 Emergency Procedures in the Florida State Courts," March 13, 2020; and "In re: Workgroup on the Continuity of Court Operations and Proceedings during and after COVID-19," June 15, 2020.

25. Supreme Court of Kentucky, "In re: Kentucky Court of Justice Response to COVID-19 Emergency—Health and Safety Requirements for the Expansion of Court Operations," May 15, 2020.

26. Rules Committee of the Superior Court of Connecticut, "Notice of Meeting of the Rules Committee of the Supreme Court under Practice Book Section 1–9B," March 20, 2020.

27. Hawai`i State Judiciary, "Update on Judiciary Actions in Light of COVID-19," March 5, 2020; Commonwealth of Massachusetts Supreme Judicial Court, "Order Authorizing the Use of Electronic Signatures by Attorneys and Self-Represented Parties," April 6, 2020.

28. Michigan Supreme Court State Court Administrative Office, "Re: Affixing and Use of Electronic Seals," April 29, 2020.

29. Supreme Court of Tennessee, "Order Regarding Electronic Signature," April 2, 2020.

30. Supreme Court of the State of Nevada, "Order Concerning Ongoing Administration of District Court Proceedings during COVID-19 Emergency," April 10, 2020.

31. Michigan Supreme Court, "Order Expanding Authority for Judicial Officers to Conduct Proceedings Remotely," April 7, 2020; Supreme Court of Missouri, "In re: Response to the Coronavirus Disease (COVID-19) Pandemic," March 16, 2020; Supreme Court of Tennessee, "In re: COVID-19 Pandemic," April 24, 2020 (first appeared in March 13, 2020, order); Supreme Court of Texas, "First Emergency Order regarding the COVID-19 State of Disaster," March 13, 2020.

32. Supreme Court of Alabama, "Administrative Order Suspending All In-Person Court Proceedings for the Next Thirty Days," March 13, 2020; Supreme Court of Arkansas, "In re Response to the COVID 19 Pandemic," March 17, 2020. To note, the Arkansas Supreme Court issued a recommendation on March 13, 2020, that courts use remote technologies but included language regarding rules suspensions in the cited order.

33. Supreme Court of Florida, "In re: COVID-19 Essential and Critical Trial Court Proceedings," March 17, 2020; Supreme Court of Missouri, "In re: Response to the Coronavirus Disease (COVID-19) Pandemic," March 22, 2020.

34. E.g., Supreme Court of the State of Hawai`i, "In the Matter of the Judiciary's Response to the COVID-19 Outbreak: Order regarding Judiciary Operations," April 27, 2020.

35. Supreme Court of Alabama, "Resumption of In-Person Hearings Authorized after May 15, 2020, and Continued Suspension of Jury Trials until September 14, 2020," May 13, 2020.

36. Supreme Court of the State of Hawai`i, "In the Matter of the Judiciary's Response to the COVID-19 Outbreak," March 16, 2020; Commonwealth of Massachusetts Supreme Judicial Court, "Order Limiting In-Person Appearances in State Courthouses to Emergency Matters That Cannot Be Resolved through a Videoconference or Telephonic Hearing," March 17, 2020.

37. Rhode Island Supreme Court, "Executive Order: COVID-19 Pandemic Response, Continuation of Emergency Measures," April 8, 2020.

38. Supreme Court of Arkansas, "In re Response to the COVID-19 Pandemic," May 8, 2020.

39. E.g., Supreme Court of Florida, "In re: COVID-19 Public Health and Safety Precautions for Phase 2," May 21, 2020; Michigan Supreme Court, "Continued Status Quo Court Operations and Phased Return to Full Court Operations," May 6, 2020.

40. Indiana Supreme Court, "In the Matter of Administrative Rule 17 Emergency Relief for Indiana Trial Courts relating to the 2019 Novel Coronavirus (COVID-19)," March 23, 2020.

41. E.g., Supreme Court of Texas, "Seventeenth Emergency Order regarding the COVID-19 State of Disaster," May 26, 2020.

42. Virginia was the first state to codify RON, in 2010. Prior to the pandemic, an additional twenty-one states had a RON provision enacted into law with courts in various stages of implementation. Bob Jawarowski, "Remote Online Notarization: More States, including New Jersey, Join the Crowd," Holland & Knight Alerts, April 17, 2020, hklaw.com/en/in sights/publications/2020/04/remote-online-notarization-more-states-in cluding-new-jersey. Washington, DC, amended its document verification processes in 2011 in response to the passage of the Uniform Unsworn Foreign Declaration Act of 2010, allowing "parties to file declarations that have not been notarized." See Superior Court Civil Rule 9-I, https://www .dccourts.gov/sites/default/files/rules-superior-court/Civil%20Rule%20 9-I.%20Verifications%2C%20Affidavits%2C%20and%20Declarations .pdf. See also New Mexico Rules of Civil Procedure for the District Courts 1–011, "Signing of Pleadings, Motions, and Other Papers; Sanctions; Unsworn Affirmations under Penalty of Perjury," https://www2.nmcourts.gov /newface/new/dmanual/pdf/05CVProcedures.pdf.

43. RON authorizations were often promulgated by bodies other than courts. E.g., Rhode Island Supreme Court, "Notarial acts shall be governed by the Remote Online Notarization guidelines promulgated by the Secretary of State," May 15, 2020; Mississippi Governor's Proclamation, "An alternative to the in-person physical presence requirement under the current notarial process is a necessary measure to combat the COVID-19 emergency . . . and allows notaries public commissioned under the laws of this State to perform a notarization for a principal not in the physical presence of the notary public," April 6 2020. On file with author. For an overview of the implementation of RON, see generally Jeffrey Page and Sun Lee, "E-signatures and Remote Online Notarization," March 1, 2021, https://www .ballardspahr.com/insights/alerts-and-articles/2021/01/e-sig-remote -online-notarization.

44. Rhode Island Supreme Court, "Executive Order: COVID-19 Pandemic Response—Continuation of Emergency Measures," April 8, 2020.

45. Vermont Supreme Court, "Order Promulgating Amendments to Administrative Order No. 49," April 6, 2020, and April 30, 2020.

46. Michigan Supreme Court State Court Administrative Office, "Re: Remote Notarization," April 20, 2020; Supreme Court of Missouri, "In re:

Emergency Procedures for the Administering of Oaths and Affirmations during the COVID-19 Pandemic," March 25, 2020.

47. Supreme Court of Ohio, "In re Notary Requirements for Domestic-Relations, Juvenile, General, and Probate Forms," June 8, 2020.

48. Supreme Court of Arkansas, "Statement on the Novel Coronavirus Outbreak (COVID-19) and the Courts," March 6, 2020.

49. Chief Justice of Kentucky, "Reopening Task Forces Will Prepare Courts to Resume Limited In-Person Services," May 1, 2020.

50. Supreme Court of the State of Hawai`i, "Order regarding the Committee on Operational Solutions," April 17, 2020; Supreme Court of Florida, "In re: Workgroup on the Continuity of Court Operations and Proceedings during and after COVID-19," April 21, 2020.

51. Supreme Court of the State of Nevada, "Order Concerning Implementation by Justice Courts of Governor's Emergency Direction 008," March 31, 2020.

52. E.g., Michigan State Court Administrative Office, "Michigan Trial Courts Virtual Courtroom Standards and Guidelines," April 7, 2020.

53. Joint statement of State Court Administrative Office, the Michigan Association of County Clerks, and the Michigan Association of Counties, "Courts, Counties, Clerks Commit to Cooperation," March 25, 2020; Chief Justice of Kentucky, "Update for March 17, 2020."

54. Supreme Court of Arkansas, "In re Response to the COVID-19 Pandemic," March 17, 2020.

55. Utah Supreme Court, "In re: Order for Court Operations during Pandemic," March 13, 2020.

56. Utah Supreme Court and the Utah Judicial Council, "Administrative Order for Court Operations during Pandemic," May 11, 2020.

57. Utah Supreme Court and the Utah Judicial Council, "Administrative Order for Court Operations during Pandemic," June 26, 2020.

58. Iowa Judicial Branch, "Coronavirus: Frequently Asked Questions," March 12, 2020.

59. Iowa Supreme Court, "In the Matter of Ongoing Provisions for Coronavirus/COVID-19 Impact Order on Court Services," March 28, 2020.

Chapter 3. The View from Below

1. The perception of monitoring may also lead agents to engage in strategic forms of compliance, selectively complying in order to preserve local independence and resources given the challenges of managing higher administrative burdens (VanSlyke 2007; see also in the adjudicatory context, e.g., Westerland et al. 2010).

2. This phenomenon is not relegated to the study of courts; scholars of public bureaucracy have also lamented the difficulties inherent in study-

ing these competing pressures given the nature of empirical research (see generally Jewell and Glaser 2006).

3. Of course, this is not an exhaustive overview of the benefits of interviewing as a research method. See Mosley (2013) for a comprehensive treatment of the subject.

4. Determined using data from the NCSC's 2016 administration of the SCO survey, as archived by Weinstein-Tull (2020).

5. They are also relatively similar with respect to their civil caseloads—the states are close to the median number of incoming civil cases per 100,000 residents and are less than one-third of a standard deviation away from one another on this measure. That said, caseload statistics may be misleading measures of case volume given variation in reporting requirements and standards across states; hence, this statistic is not a central consideration for selecting study states (for a comprehensive discussion, see Shanahan et al. 2022b).

6. Target states were selected *before* I reached out to personal and professional connections—these connections did not influence the selection of the case study states.

7. The anonymization of the states in the text serves to uphold the confidentiality of the participants' identities, given that their statements could potentially be interpreted as unfavorable to their employers or positions.

8. Conversely, judges and administrators with misaligned administrative philosophies that worked in wealthier jurisdictions tended to resist attempts made by central actors to apply technological tools consistently across jurisdictions.

Chapter 4. Beyond Emergencies

1. For applications in other sectors, see Andersson and Ostrom (2008), Ayres and Braithwaite (1992), Brodkin (1995), Lipsky (1980), and Oates (1972, 1999).

2. See appendix A for an overview of the variation in statewide and individual court-level access to electronic filing systems in "Self-Represented E-Filing: Surveying the Accessible Implementations," National Center for State Courts, July 2022, https://www.ncsc.org/__data/assets /pdf_file/0022/76432/SRL-efiling.pdf. See also Supreme Court of New Hampshire, "Second Renewed and Amended Emergency Order Governing New Hampshire Supreme Court Proceedings and Restricting Access to the Supreme Court Building," April 24, 2020; Supreme Court of Vermont, "Administrative Order No. 49: Declaration of Judicial Emergency and Changes to Court Procedures," October 5, 2020.

3. See pp. 14–15, "Michigan Trial Courts: Lessons Learned from the Pandemic of 2020–2021: Findings, Best Practices, and Recommendations,"

State Court Administrative Office Lessons Learned Committee, November 19, 2021, https://www.courts.michigan.gov/4afc1e/siteassets/COVID/lessons-learned/final-report-lessons-learned-findings-best-practices-and-recommendations-111921.pdf.

4. Even though judicial administration is delegated to Congress in the Constitution, Congress delegated much of this authority to the federal courts via the Rules Enabling Act (see Breyer 1996, 91). The process is as follows: Proposed amendments are considered by an advisory and a permanent rules committee, who seek out public feedback during a period of notice and comment. If the proposed rules do not require much revision, they are then transmitted by the permanent committee to the Judicial Conference. The conference meets yearly and transmits approved amendments to the Supreme Court, which then has the authority to approve and send the amendments to Congress. If Congress does not take action on the amendments (e.g., it votes to reject them), they take effect seven months after they are submitted to Congress (US Courts, "About the Rulemaking Process," https://bit.ly/3w5PE04, accessed August 3, 2022).

5. What happens between the proposal, initial drafting stages, and the promulgation of an approved rule can vary quite a bit by state. For example, some states allow the public to participate in the process, either through participation in or observation of rulemaking advisory committees or through public notice-and-comment periods (see generally Clopton 2018, appendixes A, B). Other supreme courts directly engage with standing advisory bodies that both advance proposals of their own volition and respond to requests from supreme courts to reconsider extant rules in light of changes to statutes or in response to procedural experiments states have undertaken. For a more detailed explanation of the different methods, see Clopton (2018), especially pp. 9–11.

6. Assessing the magnitude of these changes within and across states falls outside the project's scope. See generally Stephen Burbank, "Implementing Procedural Change: Who, How, Why, and When?" *Alabama Law Review* 49 (1997): 221–250, quoted in David Engstrom, "Digital Civil Procedure," *University of Pennsylvania Law Review* 169 (2022): 2243–2289.

7. Supreme Court of Vermont, "Re: Seventh Amendment to Administrative Order No. 49—Declaration of Judicial Emergency and Changes to Court Procedures & Miscellaneous Information," April 13, 2020.

8. Supreme Court of Florida, "In re: Amendments to Florida Rules of Civil Procedure, Florida Rules of General Practice and Judicial Administration, Florida Rules of Criminal Procedure, Florida Probate Rules, Florida Rules of Traffic Court, Florida Small Claims Rules, and Florida Rules of Appellate Procedure," July 14, 2022.

9. E.g., the state of New Jersey implemented an expansion of its e-filing system "sooner than expected" due to the effects of the COVID-19 pandemic. The system extends e-filing access for self-represented litigants in

select case types within the family, civil, small claims, and housing dockets. It also increases attorney access to e-filing in some of these areas. See JEDS User Guide, New Jersey Courts, https://www.njcourts.gov/selfhelp/jeds _user_guide.html, accessed August 1, 2022; and Suzette Parmley, "Judiciary Expands E-Filing to Deal with COVID-19," *New Jersey Law Journal*, https://www.law.com/njlawjournal/2020/04/09/judiciary-expands-e-fil ing-to-deal-with-COVID-19/, accessed August 1, 2022.

10. Supreme Court of Vermont, "Re: Nineteenth Amendment to Administrative Order No. 49—Declaration of Judicial Emergency and Changes to Court Procedures," December 22, 2020; Supreme Court of Florida, "Guidance and Best Practice Materials," June 16, 2020.

11. As one example, Utah updated its Rules of Civil Procedure to allow for alternative forms of service in 2001, including "electronic means." Utah provides a list of acceptable alternative service options on its courts website (https://www.utcourts.gov/howto/service/alternate_service.html), which can be requested via motion if traditional methods of service are ineffective. The list includes an online legal publication, text messaging, e-mail, and social media (Facebook and Twitter). Such options have been made available to litigants since 2010.

12. Vermont Judiciary, "2020 Vermont Rules for Electronic Filing," pg. 3, July 15, 2020.

13. See generally, Vermont Judiciary, "2020 Vermont Rules for Electronic Filing," July 15, 2020.

14. Vermont Supreme Court, "Order Promulgating Amendments to Rules 5, 6(a)(4), 29, and 79.1 of the Vermont Rules of Civil Procedure," May 9, 2022.

15. Vermont Supreme Court, "Emergency Order Amending Rules 2, 4, and 11 of the 2020 Vermont Rules for Electronic Filing," March 15, 2021.

16. E.g., Shelby County, Ohio, "Common Pleas Court e-Filing," March 17, 2022.

17. Ohio Supreme Court, "Amendments to the Ohio Rules of Practice and Procedure," July 1, 2022.

18. Michigan Court Rules, "Rule 2.107: Service and Filing of Pleadings and Other Documents," August 10, 2022.

19. Michigan Court Rules, "Rule 2.107."

20. Supreme Court of Florida, "In re: Amendments to Florida Rules of Civil Procedure 1.070 and 1.650," January 19, 2023; Indiana Supreme Court, "Order Amending Indiana Rules of Trial Procedure," October 29, 2021.

21. Indiana Supreme Court, "Order Amending Indiana Rules of Trial Procedure," October 29, 2021; see also Ohio Supreme Court, "Amendments to the Ohio Rules of Practice and Procedure," July 1, 2022.

22. Texas Supreme Court, "Texas Rules of Civil Procedure," no date; see also Supreme Court of Florida, "In re: Amendments to Florida Rules of

Civil Procedure, Florida Rules of General Practice and Judicial Administration, Florida Rules of Criminal Procedure, Florida Probate Rules, Florida Rules of Traffic Court, Florida Small Claims Rules, and Florida Rules of Appellate Procedure," July 14, 2022.

23. Florida Rules, "Chapter 2022-190: Committee Substitute for Senate Bill No. 1062," June 2022.

24. See pp. 34-44, Florida Bar, the Civil Procedure Rules Committee of the Florida Bar, Agenda, June 23, 2022, https://www-media.floridabar.org/uploads/2020/03/CivPRC-June-Agenda-1.pdf.

25. See p. 1, Supreme Court of Hawai`i, "Final Report of the Task Force on Civil Justice Improvements," July 24, 2019, https://www.courts.state.hi.us/wp-content/uploads/2019/08/Final-Report-of-the-Task-Force-on-Civil-Justice-Improvements.pdf.

26. Hawai`i Rules of the Circuit Courts, "Rule 4: Parties without Counsel," October 8, 2020.

27. Ohio Task Force on Improving Court Operations Using Remote Technology, "Report and Recommendations," iCourt Volume I of II, 2022, https://www.supremecourt.ohio.gov/docs/Boards/iCourt/Report VolumeI.pdf.

28. Ohio Supreme Court, "Amendments to the Ohio Rules of Practice and Procedure," July 1, 2022.

29. E.g., Michigan Chief Justice McCormack, "The new normal will not be the old normal." "Talk Justice, and LSC Podcast, Episode 5: 'How the Pandemic Is Transforming the Courts and the Legal Industry,'" Legal Services Corporation, October 16, 2020, https://www.lsc.gov/press-release/talk-justice-lsc-podcast-episode-5-how-pandemic-transforming-courts-and-legal; Georgia Chief Justice Nahmias, "Virtual proceedings are one of the lessons learned from the pandemic that will be used long after it dissipates." AP, "Georgia Chief Justice: Virtual Hearings Here to Stay," AP News, February 8, 2022, https://apnews.com/article/georgia-judiciary-bbbb148ebd4d19d6daad0867d60733d0; Minnesota Chief Justice Gildea, "The purpose of the presumptive format standards is to provide statewide consistency for parties and district courts." Barbara L. Jones, "Remote Hearings Are Here to Stay, Chief Justice Tells Bar Convention," June 30, 2022, https://minnlawyer.com/2022/06/30/remote-hearings-are-here-to-stay-chief-justice-tells-bar-convention/; Florida Chief Justice Canady, "Our response to the pandemic will forever change the way Florida's courts operate. Our new ways of doing things have been welcomed by attorneys and are very popular with many of those who come to the courts. Remote proceedings are here to stay." Florida Supreme Court, "Chief Justice Canady Says Florida's Courts Are Working, Responding," January 27, 2021, https://supremecourt.flcourts.gov/News-Media/Court-News/Chief-Justice-Canady-says-Florida-s-courts-are-working-responding; Illinois Chief Justice Theis, "The COVID-19 pandemic changed the way our courts

operate and remote proceedings are here to stay." Illinois Courts, "Supreme Court Amends Rules on Remote Court Appearances," no date, https://www.illinoiscourts.gov/News/1183/Supreme-Court-amends-rules-on-remote-court-appearances/news-detail/; Texas Chief Justice Nathan Hecht, "I think a lot of these changes are here to stay." Meera Gajjar, "'The American Justice System Will Never Be the Same,' Says Texas Supreme Court Chief Justice Nathan Hecht," Thomson Reuters, April 24, 2020, https://www.thomsonreuters.com/en-us/posts/news-and-media/texas-supreme-court-chief-justice-nathan-hecht/.

30. Vermont Supreme Court, "Order Promulgating Amendments to Rule 6 of the Vermont Rules of Small Claims Procedure and Rule 80.6 of the Vermont Rules of Civil Procedure," September 13, 2022.

31. Vermont's current Rule 43.1, to which this rule refers, was originally promulgated in 2019 and includes language regarding the considerations a judge should take into account when making a determination about hearing modality. The court established a committee to propose permanent rule changes for remote court proceedings in response to the pandemic, and the proposed further amendments to Rule 43.1 resulting from its study of the experiences of those involved with fully remote and hybrid proceedings. The proposed rule contains different standards for evidentiary and nonevidentiary proceedings, introduces the concepts of remote and hybrid proceedings, and allows judges to schedule remote or hybrid participation for nonevidentiary proceedings while requiring a determination of good cause for evidentiary proceedings. The amended rule would also provide for waivers of time and notice requirements in certain circumstances and includes factors for the court to consider when determining good cause for remote or hybrid evidentiary proceedings. At the time of writing, these changes are still pending. See https://www.vermontjudiciary.org/sites/default/files/documents/PROPOSED-VRCP43.1—FOR%20COMMENT.pdf, accessed February 13, 2023.

32. Supreme Court of Florida, "In re: Amendments to Florida Rules of Civil Procedure, Florida Rules of General Practice and Judicial Administration, Florida Rules of Criminal Procedure, Florida Probate Rules, Florida Rules of Traffic Court, Florida Small Claims Rules, and Florida Rules of Appellate Procedure," July 14, 2022.

33. Vermont Supreme Court, "Order Promulgating Amendments to Rule 6 of the Vermont Rules of Small Claims Procedure and Rule 80.6 of the Vermont Rules of Civil Procedure," September 13, 2022; see also Indiana Court Rules, "Indiana Administrative Rules: Interim Rule 14—Remote Proceedings," September 30, 2022.

34. Supreme Court of Florida, "In re: Amendments to Florida Rules," July 14, 2022.

35. Hawaiʻi State Judiciary, "Rule 16.2—Appearance by Telephone of Video Conference Call," January 12, 2023.

36. Superior Court of Massachusetts, "Standing Order 1–22: Videoconferencing of Court Events," August 12, 2022.

37. Supreme Court of Florida, "In re: Amendments to Florida Rules," July 14, 2022.

38. Michigan Court Rules, "Rule 2.408: Use of Videoconferencing Technology in Civil Cases," August 10, 2022.

39. Michigan Supreme Court, "Retention of the July 26, 2021 Amendments," McCormack, C.J., concurring, 16–17, August 10, 2022.

40. "Factors. In determining good cause under this rule, the court should consider factors such as: (1) case type; (2) court proceeding type; (3) the number of parties and witnesses; (4) the complexity of the legal and factual issues; (5) the type of evidence to be submitted, if any; (6) technological restrictions such as lack of access to or proficiency in necessary technology; (7) travel restrictions such as lack of transportation, distance, or inability to take off work; (8) whether a method of appearance is best suited to provide necessary language access services for a person with limited English proficiency or accommodations for a person with a disability; and (9) any previous abuse of a method of appearance." Texas Supreme Court, "Texas Rules of Civil Procedure: Rule 21d—Appearances at Court Proceedings," 2023, https://www.txcourts.gov/media/1455531/texas-rules-of-civil-procedure.pdf.

Conclusion: Power Dynamics and Administrative Capacity

1. For a national review of such programs, see Treskon et al. 2021.

2. Michigan Governor's Office, "Governor Whitmer Signs Bill for Supplemental Funding to Support COVID-19 Response," news release, July 1, 2020, https://www.michigan.gov/coronavirus/news/2020/07/01/governor-whitmer-signs-bill-for-supplemental-funding-to-support-COVID-19-response.

3. Texas Governor's Office, "Governor Abbott Announces over $171 Million in CARES Act Funding for Rental Assistance, Texas Eviction Diversion Program," news release, September 25, 2020, https://gov.texas.gov/news/post/governor-abbott-announces-over-171-million-in-cares-act-funding-for-rental-assistance-texas-eviction-diversion-program.

4. Michigan Supreme Court, "Priority Treatment and New Procedure for Landlord/Tenant Cases," June 24, 2020.

5. See, e.g., Supreme Court of Texas, "Thirty-Ninth Emergency Order Regarding the COVID-19 State of Disaster," July 19, 2021.

6. Supreme Court of Illinois, "Illinois Courts Response to COVID-19 Emergency/Eviction Early Resolution Programs," February 23, 2021.

7. Kentucky Courts, "Chief Justice Minton Forms Reopening Task Forces to Prepare Courts to Resume Limited In-Person Services," May 1, 2020, https://www.kentucky.gov/Pages/Activity-stream.aspx?n=Kentucky CourtofJustice&prId=175.

8. Supreme Court of Hawai`i, "Order Regarding the Committee on Operational Solutions," April 17, 2020; Indiana Supreme Court, "Resuming Operations of the Trial Courts: COVID-19 Guidelines for Indiana's Judiciary," p. 3, May 13, 2020, https://www.in.gov/courts/files/COVID19-re suming-trial-court-operations.pdf.

9. Massachusetts Access to Justice Commission, "Creating a More Equitable System: Lessons Learned during the COVID-19 Pandemic," p. 23, September 2022, https://massa2j.org/wp-content/uploads/2022/10/MA -ATJ-Commission-Report-on-Lessons-Learned-during-the-Pandemic.pdf.

10. Supreme Court of Texas, "Order Creating Remote Proceedings Task Force," December 22, 2020, https://www.txcourts.gov/media /1450174/209152.pdf.

11. Texas Supreme Court Advisory Committee, "Memorandum in Re: Proposals Relating to Remote Hearings," pp. 123–124, memo dated November 8, 2021, https://www.txcourts.gov/media/1454951/scac-meeting-note book-20220930.pdf.

12. Michigan Supreme Court, "Courts and COVID-19—Building Capacity, What You Can Do Now," April 7, 2020.

13. Florida Supreme Court, "In re: Comprehensive COVID-19 Emergency Measures for the Florida State Courts," June 8, 2020.

14. State of Vermont, Supreme Court, "Order Promulgating Amendments to Administrative Order No. 49," March 20, 2020.

15. Florida Supreme Court, "In re: Comprehensive . . . Measures," June 8, 2020; Vermont Judiciary, "2020 Vermont Rules for Electronic Filing," July 15, 2020.

16. Vermont Supreme Court, "Order Promulgating Amendments to Rules 43.1 of the Vermont Rules of Civil Procedure, Proposed," 2023.

17. An initial version of the rule change was proposed in 2022, with comments requested by early 2023. A revised version of the rule was open for comments through late February 2024. See reporter's notes (draft), "Massachusetts Rules of Civil Procedure, Rule 11. Appearances and Pleadings, Proposed Amendment," 2023; and "Massachusetts Rules of Civil Procedure, Rule 11. Appearances and Pleadings; Signatures," 2024. On file with author and available for download at https://masslawyersweekly .com/wp-content/blogs.dir/1/files/2024/01/notice-inviting-comment -on-proposed-amendments-to-mass-r-civ-p-11-draft-reporter-notes-febru ary-2024.docx.pdf.

18. Supreme Court of Arizona, "In the Matter of: Authorizing Limitation of Court Operations during a Public Health Emergency and Transition to Resumption of Certain Operations," May 20, 2020.

19. Supreme Court of Georgia, "Second Order Extending Declaration of Statewide Judicial Emergency," May 11, 2020.

20. This paragraph offers the smallest of samples of the wide range of activities undertaken by these different researchers and institutions. For one organization's comprehensive repository of post-pandemic resources, visit the National Center for State Courts "Pandemic-Era Resources for Courts" webpage, https://www.ncsc.org/consulting-and-research/areas-of -expertise/court-management-and-performance/pandemic-and-the -courts-resources, accessed January 4, 2024.

References

Aberbach, Joel D., and Bert A. Rockman. 2002. "Conducting and Coding Elite Interviews." *PS: Political Science & Politics* 35 (4): 673–676.

Aikman, Alexander B. 2006. *The Art and Practice of Court Administration*. Boca Raton, FL: CRC Press.

Alexander, Charlotte S., and Lauren Sudeall. 2023. "Creating a People-First Court Data Framework." *Harvard Civil Rights-Civil Liberties Law Review* 58 (2): 731–788.

Andersson, Krister P., Clark C. Gibson, and Fabrice Lehoucq. 2006. "Municipal Politics and Forest Governance: Comparative Analysis of Decentralization in Bolivia and Guatemala." *World Development* 34 (3): 576–595.

Andersson, Krister P., and Elinor Ostrom. 2008. "Analyzing Decentralized Resource Regimes from a Polycentric Perspective." *Policy Sciences* 41 (1): 71–93.

Ansell, Chris, and Alison Gash. 2008. "Collaborative Governance in Theory and Practice." *Journal of Public Administration Research and Theory* 18 (4): 543–571.

Ansell, Christopher, Eva Sørensen, and Jacob Torfing. 2021. "The COVID-19 Pandemic as a Game Changer for Public Administration and Leadership? The Need for Robust Governance Responses to Turbulent Problems." *Public Management Review* 23 (7): 949–960.

Anthony, Robert A. 1992. "Interpretive Rules, Policy Statements, Guidances, Manuals, and the Like—Should Federal Agencies Use Them to Bind the Public?" *Duke Law Journal* 41 (6): 1311–1384.

Arbuthnot, Jack. 2002. "A Call Unheeded: Courts' Perceived Obstacles to Establishing Divorce Education Programs." *Family Court Review* 40 (3): 371–382.

Atkinson, Rowland, and John Flint. 2001. "Accessing Hidden and Hard-to-Reach Populations: Snowball Research Strategies." *Social Research Update* 33 (1): 1–4.

Avraham, Ronen, and William HJ Hubbard. 2022. "Civil Procedure as the Regulation of Externalities." *The University of Chicago Law Review* 89 (1): 1–64.

Ayres, Ian, and John Braithwaite. 1992. "Partial-Industry Regulation: A Monopsony Standard for Consumer Protection." *California Law Review* 80 (1): 13–53.

Bannon, Alicia, and Janna Adelstein. 2020. "The Impact of Video Proceedings on Fairness and Access to Justice in Court." New York: Brennan Center for Justice at New York University School of Law, September 10.

Bannon, Alicia L., and Douglas Keith. 2020. "Remote Court: Principles for Virtual Proceedings during the COVID-19 Pandemic and Beyond." *Northwestern University Law Review* 115 (6): 1875–1920.

Bardach, Eugene, and Robert A. Kagan. 1982. *Going by the Book: The Problem of Regulatory Unreasonableness.* Philadelphia: Temple University Press.

Barton, Benjamin H. 2010. "Against Civil Gideon (and for Pro Se Court Reform)." *Florida Law Review* 62 (4): 1228–1274.

Bazemore, Gordon. 1998. "Crime Victims and Restorative Justice in Juvenile Courts: Judges as Obstacle or Leader?" *Western Criminology Review* 1 (1): [online].

Behn, Robert D. 2001. *Rethinking Democratic Accountability.* Washington, DC: Brookings Institution Press.

Beim, Deborah. 2017. "Learning in the Judicial Hierarchy." *Journal of Politics* 79 (2): 591–604.

Benesh, Sara C., and Malia Reddick. 2002. "Overruled: An Event History Analysis of Lower Court Reaction to Supreme Court Alteration of Precedent." *Journal of Politics* 64 (2): 534–550.

Benfer, Emily A., Robert Koehler, Alyx Mark, Valerie Nazzaro, Anne Kat Alexander, Peter Hepburn, Danya E. Keene, and Matthew Desmond. 2022. "COVID-19 Housing Policy: State and Federal Eviction Moratoria and Supportive Measures in the United States During the Pandemic." *Housing Policy Debate*: 1–25.

Benfer, Emily A., David Vlahov, Marissa Y. Long, Evan Walker-Wells, J. L. Pottenger, Gregg Gonsalves, and Danya E. Keene. 2021. "Eviction, Health Inequity, and the Spread of COVID-19: Housing Policy as a Primary Pandemic Mitigation Strategy." *Journal of Urban Health* 98: 1–12.

Berkson, Larry, and Steven W. Hays. 1976. "Injecting Court Administrators into an Old System: A Case of Conflict in Florida." *Justice System Journal*: 57–76.

Bingham, Andrea J., and Patricia Witkowsky. 2021. "Deductive and Inductive Approaches to Qualitative Data Analysis." In *Analyzing and Interpreting Qualitative Data: After the Interview*, edited by C. Vanover, P. Mihas, and J. Saldaña, 133–146. Thousand Oaks, CA: Sage.

Bone, Robert G. 2007. "Who Decides—A Critical Look at Procedural Discretion." *Cardozo Law Review* 28 (5): 1961–2024.

Bookman, Pamela K., and Colleen F. Shanahan. 2022. "A Tale of Two Civil Procedures." *Columbia Law Review* 122: 1183–1242.

Bookman, Pamela K., and David L. Noll. 2017. "Ad Hoc Procedure." *New York University Law Review* 92 (4): 767–845.

Bowie, Jennifer, and Elisha Carol Savchak. 2019. "Understanding the Determinants of Opinion Language Borrowing in State Courts in the

United States." In *Research Handbook on Law and Courts*, edited by Susan M. Sterett and Lee D. Walker, 267–279. Northampton, UK: Edward Elgar.

Boyd, Christina L. 2015. "The Hierarchical Influence of Courts of Appeals on District Courts." *Journal of Legal Studies* 44(1): 113–141.

Boyd, Christina L., and Adam G. Rutkowski. 2020. "Trial Courts in the United States." In *Oxford Research Encyclopedia of Politics*. Oxford: Oxford University Press.

Boyd, Christina L., and James F. Spriggs. 2009. "An Examination of Strategic Anticipation of Appellate Court Preferences by Federal District Court Judges." *Washington University Journal of Law and Policy* 29: 37–82.

Bozeman, Barry, and Patrick Scott. 1996. "Bureaucratic Red Tape and Formalization: Untangling Conceptual Knots." *American Review of Public Administration* 26 (1): 1–17.

Braun, Virginia, and Victoria Clarke. 2006. "Using Thematic Analysis in Psychology." *Qualitative Research in Psychology* 3 (2): 77–101.

Breyer, Stephen G. 1996. "Judicial Independence in the United States." *St. Louis University Law Journal* 40 (Summer): 989–996.

Brinkman, Michelle. 2007. "A Study of Community Fair Cross-Section Representation of the Jury Venire in Travis County, Texas under the I-Jury Process." Report, Institute for Court Management, National Center for State Courts, Williamsburg, VA.

Brodkin, Evelyn Z. 1995. "The War against Welfare." *Dissent* 42 (2): 211–220.

Buenger, Michael L. 2020. "Rethinking the Delivery of Justice in a Self-Service Society." *Journal of Dispute Resolution*: 109–120.

Bulinski, Maximilian A., and J. J. Prescott. 2015. "Online Case Resolution Systems: Enhancing Access, Fairness, Accuracy, and Efficiency." *Michigan Journal of Race and Law* 21 (2): 205–250.

Burbank, Steven B., and Sean Farhang. 2014. "Class Actions and the Counterrevolution against Federal Litigation." *University of Pennsylvania Law Review* 165 (7): 1495–1530.

———. 2017. "Litigation Reform: An Institutional Approach." *University of Pennsylvania Law Review* 162 (7): 1543–1618.

Butler, Paul. 2013. "Poor People Lose: Gideon and the Critique of Rights." *Yale Law Journal* 122: 2176–2204.

Cabral, James E., Abhijeet Chavan, Thomas M. Clarke, and John Greacen. 2012. "Using Technology to Enhance Access to Justice." *Harvard Journal of Law and Technology* 26: 241–324.

Caldeira, Gregory A., and John Wright. 1988. "Organized Interests and Agenda Setting in the U.S. Supreme Court." *American Political Science Review* 82 (4): 1109–1127.

Cameron, Charles M. 1993. "New Avenues for Modeling Judicial Politics." Paper presented at the Conference on the Political Economy of Public Law, Rochester, NY.

Cappellina, Bartolomeo, Anne Ausfelder, Adam Eick, Romain Mespoulet, Miriam Hartlapp, Sabine Saurugger, and Fabien Terpan. 2022. "Ever More Soft Law? A Dataset to Compare Binding and Non-Binding EU Law across Policy Areas and Over Time (2004–2019)." *European Union Politics* 23 (4): 741–757.

Carpenter, Anna E., Alyx Mark, Colleen F. Shanahan, and Jessica K. Steinberg. 2022a. "The Field of State Civil Courts." *Columbia Law Review* 122: 1165–1182.

Carpenter, Anna E., Colleen F. Shanahan, Jessica K. Steinberg, and Alyx Mark. 2022b. "Judges in Lawyerless Courts." *Georgetown Law Journal* 110 (3): 509–567.

Carpenter, Anna E., Jessica K. Steinberg, Colleen F. Shanahan, and Alyx Mark. 2018. "Studying the New Civil Judges." *Wisconsin Law Review* 2018 (2): 249–286.

CCJ/COSCA. 2020. "Resolution 2 in Support of the Guiding Principles for Post-Pandemic Court Technology." July 2020. https://ccj.ncsc.org/__data/assets/pdf_file/0019/51193/Resolution-2-In-Support-of-the-Guiding-Principles-for-Post-Pandemic-Court-Technology-.pdf.

———. 2021. "Resolution 3: In Support of Process Simplification." July. https://ccj.ncsc.org/__data/assets/pdf_file/0017/67013/Resolution-3_Process-Simplification.pdf.

Centers for Disease Control and Prevention. 2022. "COVID-19 Vaccination for Children." October 2022. https://www.cdc.gov/vaccines/covid-19/planning/children.html.

Clarke, Victoria, and Virginia Braun. 2013. "Teaching Thematic Analysis." *Psychologist* 26 (2): 120–133.

Clopton, Zachary D. 2018. "Making State Civil Procedure." *Cornell Law Review* 104 (1): 1–100.

Cole, David. 1999. *No Equal Justice: Race and Class in the American Criminal Justice System.* New York: New Press.

Coleman, Brooke D. 2018. "#SOWHITEMALE: Federal Civil Rulemaking." *Northwestern University Law Review* 113 (2): 407–431.

Conference of Chief Justices and Conference of State Court Administrators. 2006. "Resolution 13: The Emergence of E-Everything." https://ccj.ncsc.org/__data/assets/pdf_file/0011/23420/01182006-the-emergence-of-e-everything.pdf.

———. 2021. "Resolution 2: In Support of the Guiding Principles for Post-Pandemic Court Technology." https://ccj.ncsc.org/__data/assets/pdf_file/0019/51193/Resolution-2-In-Support-of-the-GuidingPrinciples-for-Post-Pandemic-Court-Technology-.pdf.

Corso, Joseph W. 1979. "Three Political Theories for Court Administrators." *Judicature* 63 (9): 427–435.

Court Statistics Project of the National Center for State Courts. 2016. "State Court Organization." Dataset. National Center for State Courts.

Decker, Annie. 2014. "A Theory of Local Common Law." *Cardozo Law Review* 35: 1939—1992.

DeHart Davis, Leisha. 2007. "The Unbureaucratic Personality." *Public Administration Review* 67 (5): 892-903.

DiMaggio, Paul. 1988. "Interest and Agency in Institutional Theory." In *Research on Institutional Patterns: Environment and Culture,* edited by L. G. Zucker, 3-21. Pensacola, FL: Ballinger.

Emerson, Kirk, and Tina Nabatchi. 2015. *Collaborative Governance Regimes.* Washington, DC: Georgetown University Press.

Epstein, Lee, Jack Knight, and Andrew D. Martin. 2003. "The Norm of Prior Judicial Experience and Its Consequences for Career Diversity on the U.S. Supreme Court." *California Law Review* 91 (4): 903-965.

Farley, Erin J., Elise Jensen, and Michael Rempel. 2014. "Improving Courtroom Communication: A Procedural Justice Experience in Milwaukee." Report, Center for Court Innovation, New York, NY.

Ferner, Anthony, and Paul Edwards. 1995. "Power and the Diffusion of Organizational Change within Multinational Enterprises." *European Journal of Industrial Relations* 1 (2): 229-257.

Fleming, Casey J. 2020. "Prosocial Rule Breaking at the Street Level: The Roles of Leaders, Peers, and Bureaucracy." *Public Management Review* 22 (8): 1191-1216.

Friedman, Barry, and Erwin Chemerinsky. 1995. "The Fragmentation of the Federal Rules." *Judicature* 79: 67-73.

Galanter, Marc. 1974. "Why the Haves Come Out Ahead: Speculations on the Limits of Legal Change." *Law & Society Review* 9: 95-160.

Gallas, Geoff. 1976. "The Conventional Wisdom of State Court Administration: A Critical Assessment and an Alternative Approach." *Justice System Journal* 2: 35-56.

Gerring, John, and Lee Cojocaru. 2016. "Selecting Cases for Intensive Analysis: A Diversity of Goals and Methods." *Sociological Methods & Research* 45 (3): 392-423.

Gofen, Anat. 2015. "Reconciling Policy Dissonance: Patterns of Governmental Response to Policy Noncompliance." *Policy Sciences* 48 (1): 3-24.

Gold, Sara, Toby Treem Guerin, and Kerri McGowan Lowrey. 2022. "A Holistic Approach to Eviction Prevention during the COVID-19 Pandemic: Challenge and Opportunities for the Future." *Washington University Journal of Law and Policy* 68: 183-214.

Goldstein, Kenneth. 2002. "Getting in the Door: Sampling and Completing Elite Interviews." *PS: Political Science & Politics* 35 (4): 669-672.

Gormley, William T., and Steven J. Balla. 2004. *Bureaucracy and Democracy: Accountability and Performance.* Washington, DC: CQ Press.

Gough, Brendan, and Anna Madill. 2012. "Subjectivity in Psychological Science: From Problem to Prospect." *Psychological Methods* 17 (3): 374-384.

Grossback, Lawrence J., Sean Nicholson-Crotty, David A. M. Peterson. 2004. "Ideology and Learning in Policy Diffusion." *American Politics Research* 32 (5): 521–545.

Guzman, Andrew T., and Timothy L. Meyer. 2010. "International Soft Law." *Journal of Legal Analysis* 2 (1): 171–225.

Hannaford-Agor, Paula. 2003. "Court Review: Volume 39, Issue 4—Helping the Pro Se Litigant: A Changing Landscape." *Court Review: The Journal of the American Judges Association*: 8–16.

Hedge, David M., and Michael J. Scicchitano. 1994. "Regulating in Space and Time: The Case of Regulatory Federalism." *Journal of Politics* 56 (1): 134–153.

Henderson, Thomas A. 1984. *The Significance of Judicial Structure: The Effect of Unification on Trial Court Operations.* Washington, DC: US Department of Justice, National Institute of Justice.

Hershkoff, Helen. 2001. "State Courts and the Passive Virtues: Rethinking the Judicial Function." *Harvard Law Review* 114 (7), 1833–1942.

Hochschild, Jennifer L. 2009. "Conducting Intensive Interviews and Elite Interviews." Memorandum, Workshop on Interdisciplinary Standards for Systematic Qualitative Research.

Hoffman, David A., and Anton Strezhnev. 2023. "Longer trips to court cause evictions." *Proceedings of the National Academy of Sciences* 120 (2): 1-11.

Hooghe, Liesbet, and Gary Marks. 2009. "A Postfunctionalist Theory of European Integration: From Permissive Consensus to Constraining." *British Journal of Political Science* 39 (1): 1–23.

Jewell, Christopher J., and Bonnie E. Glaser. 2006. "Toward a General Analytic Framework: Organizational Settings, Policy Goals, and Street-Level Behavior." *Administration & Society* 38 (3): 335–364.

Johnson, Donald. 2014. *Judicial Attitudes Regarding Court Records Transparency.* PhD diss., University of Southern Mississippi.

JTC. 2020. "Quick Response Bulletin: Judicial Perspectives on ODR and Other Virtual Court Processes Version 1.0." May. https://www.ncsc.org /_data/assets/pdf_file/0018/42912/2020-07-27-Judicial-Perspectives-002.pdf.

Kim, Pauline T., Margo Schlanger, Christina L. Boyd, and Andrew D. Martin. 2009. "How Should We Study District Judge Decision-Making?" *Washington University Journal of Law and Policy* 29: 83–112.

Klein, Susan R. 1999. "Redrawing the Criminal-Civil Boundary." *Buffalo Criminal Law Review* 2 (2): 681–723.

Koppel, Glenn S. 2005. "Toward a New Federalism in State Civil Justice: Developing a Uniform Code of State Civil Procedure through a Collaborative Rule-Making Process." *Vanderbilt Law Review* 58: 1167–1278.

Kornhauser, Lewis A. 1995. "Adjudication by a Resource-Constrained

Team: Hierarchy and Precedent in a Judicial System." *Southern California Law Review* 68 (September): 1605–1630.

Krimmel, John Theodore. 1993. *An Analysis of New Jersey's Drug Court Project: A Time Series Quasi-experiment.* PhD diss., City University of New York.

Kritzer, Herbert M. 1982. "The Judge's Role in Pretrial Case Processing: Assessing the Need for Change." *Judicature* 66 (1): 28–38.

Kvale, Steinar, and Svend Brinkmann. 1996. *InterViews: Learning the Craft of Qualitative Research Interviewing.* Newbury Park, CA: Sage.

Ladha, Krishna K., and Gary Miller. 1996. "Political Discourse, Factions, and the General Will: Correlated Voting and Condorcet's Jury Theorem." In *Collective Decision-Making: Social Choice and Political Economy*, edited by Normal Schofield, 393-410. Boston: Kluwer Academic.

Lederer, Frederic I. 2021. "The Evolving Technology-Augmented Courtroom before, during, and after the Pandemic." *Vanderbilt Journal of Entertainment and Technology Law* 23 (2): 301-339.

Lee, Cynthia G., F. Cheesman, D. Rottman, Rachel Swaner, Suvi Lambson, Mike Rempel, and Ric Curtis. 2013. "A Community Court Grows in Brooklyn: A Comprehensive Evaluation of the Red Hook (Community Justice Center Final Report)." National Center for State Courts, Williamsburg, VA.

Lee, Don S., and Soonae Park. 2023. "Bureaucratic Responsiveness under Dynamic Political Settings: Experimental Evidence from Local Governments." *Legislative Studies Quarterly*: 1-30.

Leib, Ethan J. 2015. "Local Judges and Local Government." *NYU Journal of Legislation and Public Policy* 18 (4): 707-739.

Legal Services Corporation. 2013. "Report of the Summit on the Use of Technology to Expand Access to Justice." Report. https://www.lsc.gov/sites/default/files/LSC_Tech%20Summit%20Report_2013.pdf.

Leonetti, Carrie. 2012. "Watching the Hen House: Judicial Rulemaking and Judicial Review." *Nebraska Law Review* 91: 72-120.

Leuffen, D. 2006. "Bienvenue or Access Denied? Recruiting French Political Elites for In-Depth Interviews." *French Politics* 4: 342-347.

Levin, Leo. 1991. "Local Rules As Experiments: A Study in the Division of Power." *University of Pennsylvania Law Review* 139 (6): 1567-1596.

Lindquist, Stefanie A., and David Klein. 2006. "The Influence of Jurisprudential Considerations on Supreme Court Decisionmaking: A Study of Conflict Cases." *Law & Society Review* 40 (1): 135-162.

Linos, Katerina, and Melissa Carlson. 2017. "Qualitative Methods for Law Review Writing." *University of Chicago Law Review* 84 (1): 213-238.

Lipsky, Michael. 1980. *Street Level Bureaucracy: Dilemmas of the Individual in Public Services.* New York: Russell Sage Foundation.

Liu, Zejin, and Steven Van de Walle. 2020. "Understanding Policy Instruments for Steering Nonprofit Organizations in China: Only Carrots and

Sticks?" *VOLUNTAS: International Journal of Voluntary & Nonprofit Organizations*, 31: 736–750.

McNollgast. 1995. "Politics and the Courts: A Positive Theory of Judicial Doctrine and the Rule of Law." *Southern California Law Review* 68 (6): 1631–1689.

Main, Thomas O. 2001. "Procedural Uniformity and the Exaggerated Role of Rules: A Survey of Intra-State Uniformity in Three States That Have Not Adopted the Federal Rules of Civil Procedure." *Villanova Law Review* 46: 311–384.

———. 2014. "Civil Rulemaking in Nevada: Contemplating a New Advisory Committee." *Nevada Law Journal* 14 (3): 852–865.

Mann, Kenneth. 1991. "Punitive Civil Sanctions: The Middleground between Criminal and Civil Law." *Yale Law Journal* 101: 1795–1873.

March, James G., Martin Schulz, and Xueguang Zhou. 2000. *The Dynamics of Rules: Change in Written Organizational Codes*. Stanford, CA: Stanford University Press.

Marcus, Richard, 2013. "'American Exceptionalism' in Goals for Civil Litigation." In *Goals of Civil Justice and Civil Procedure in Contemporary Judicial Systems*, edited by Alan Uzelac, 123–141. Berlin: Springer International Publishing.

Mark, Alyx. 2024. "Pandemic Policymaking in State Supreme Courts: Implications for the Administration of Justice." *American Bar Association Judges' Journal* 63 (2): 22–27.

Mavrot, Céline, and Susanne Hadorn. 2021. "When Politicians Do Not Care for the Policy: Street-Level Compliance in Cross-Agency Contexts." *Public Policy & Administration*: 1–20.

Mays, G. Larry, and William A. Taggart. 1985. "Local Court Administration: Findings from a Survey of Appointed Managers." *Judicature* 69 (1): 29–35.

McCubbins, Matthew D., and Thomas Schwartz. 1984. "Congressional Oversight Overlooked: Police Patrols versus Fire Alarms." *American Journal of Political Science* 28 (1): 165–179.

Moskowitz, Seymour. 2002. "Rediscovering Discovery: State Procedural Rules and the Level Playing Field." *Rutgers Law Review* 54: 595–648.

Mosley, Layna. 2013. *Interview Research in Political Science*. Ithaca, NY: Cornell University Press.

Mulcahy, Linda, Emma Rowden, and Wendy Teeder. 2020. "Exploring the Case for Virtual Jury Trials during the COVID-19 Crisis: An Evaluation of a Pilot Study Conducted by JUSTICE." Report, JUSTICE, London.

Mulcahy, Linda, Emma Rowden, and Anna Tsalapatanis. 2022. "Supporting Online Justice: Enhancing Accessibility, Participation and Procedural Fairness." Report, University of Oxford Centre for Socio-legal Studies, Oxford, UK.

Mullenix, Linda S. 1991. "Problems in Complex Litigation." *Review of Litigation* 10 (2): 213-230.

National Center for State Courts. 2023. "Will Remote Hearings Improve Appearance Rates?" @ *the Center.* May. https://perma.cc/47V9-467H.

National Center for State Courts Access to Justice Team. 2023. "The Things We Think and do Not Always Say: Access to Justice Manifesto." March. https://www.ncsc.org/__data/assets/pdf_file/0035/88838/Access _To_Justice_Manifesto_.pdf.

Nazem, Samira. 2022. "Creating Post-Pandemic Eviction Court. Trends in State Courts." *Trends in State Courts:* 1-10.

Nir, Esther. 2018. "Approaching the Bench: Accessing Elites on the Judiciary for Qualitative Interviews." *International Journal of Social Research Methodology* 21 (1): 77-89.

Noy, Chaim. 2008. "Sampling Knowledge: The Hermeneutics of Snowball Sampling in Qualitative Research." *International Journal of Social Research Methodology* 11 (4): 327-344.

Oates, Wallace E. 1999. "An Essay on Fiscal Federalism." *Journal of Economic Literature* 37 (3): 1120-1149.

————. 1972. *Fiscal Federalism.* New York: Harcourt Brace Jovanovich.

Ostrom, Elinor, Larry Schroeder, and Susan Wynne. 1993. "Analyzing the Performance of Alternative Institutional Arrangements for Sustaining Rural Infrastructure in Developing Countries." *Journal of Public Administration Research and Theory* 3 (1): 11-45.

Patton, Michael Quinn. 1990. *Qualitative Research & Evaluation Methods,* 2nd ed. Newbury Park, CA: Sage.

Parrillo, Nicholas R. 2019. "Federal Agency Guidance and the Power to Bind." *Yale Journal on Regulation* 36 (1): 165-270.

Pew Charitable Trusts. 2021. "How Courts Embraced Technology, Met the Pandemic Challenge, and Revolutionized Their Operations." https://www.pewtrusts.org/en/research-and-analysis/reports/2021 /12/how-courts-embraced-technology-met-the-pandemic-chal lenge-and-revolutionized-their-operations.

————. 2023a. "How to Share Civil Justice Data with Third Parties to Improve Public Knowledge, Oversight." https://www.pewtrusts.org/-/media /assets/2023/09/courts/how-to-share-civil-justice-data-with-third-par ties-to-improve-public-knowledge-and-oversight.pdf.

————. 2023b. "How to Simplify Court Processes and Support User Engagement: A Fact Sheet from Pew." https://www.pewtrusts.org/-/media /assets/2023/12/clsm-06_how_to_simplify_court_processes_to_sup port_user_engagement_web-final.pdf.

————. 2023c. "How Organizing, Sharing Data Can Boost Court Transparency." https://www.pewtrusts.org/-/media/assets/2023/09/courts/how -organizing-and-sharing-data-can-boost-court-transparency.pdf.

Pollack, Michael C. 2021. "Courts beyond Judging." *Brigham Young University Law Review* 46 (3): 719-794.

Posner, Richard A. 2010. *How Judges Think*. Cambridge, MA: Harvard University Press.

Potts, Keagan. 2021. "A Solution to the Hard Problem of Soft Law." *Michigan Journal of Environmental & Administrative Law* 10 (2): 483-505.

Quintanilla, Victor D., Kurt Hugenberg, Margaret Hagan, Amy Gonzales, Ryan Hutchings, and Nedim Yel. 2023a. "Digital Inequalities and Access to Justice Dialing into Zoom Court Unrepresented. In *Legal Tech and Access to Justice*, edited by David Freeman Engstrom, 225-250. Cambridge: Cambridge University Press.

Quintanilla, Victor D., Kurt Hugenberg, Ryan Hutchings, and Nedim Yel. 2023b. *Accessing Justice with Zoom: Experiences and Outcomes in Online Civil Courts*. Report, University Maurer School of Law, Bloomington, IN.

Rachlinski, Jeffrey J. 2006. "Bottom-up versus Top-down Lawmaking." *University of Chicago Law Review* 73 (3): 933-964.

Raftery, William. 2013. "Unification and Bragency: A Century of Court Organization and Reorganization." *Judicature* 96 (6): 337-347.

———. 2015. "Efficiency of Unified vs. Non-Unified State Judiciaries: An Examination of Court Organizational Performance." PhD diss., Virginia Commonwealth University.

Randazzo, Kirk A. 2008. "Strategic Anticipation and the Hierarchy of Justice in US District Courts." *American Politics Research* 36 (5): 669-693.

Reda, Dana Shocair. 2017. "What Does It Mean to Say That Procedure Is Political?" *Fordham Law Review* 85: 2203-2225.

Reinhart, Christopher, and George Coppolo. 2002. "Court Rules in Other States: Legislative Approval." White paper, Connecticut Office of Legislative Research.

Resnik, Judith. 1982. "Managerial Judges." *Harvard Law Review* 96 (2): 374-448.

Richardson, L. Song, and Phillip Goff. 2013. "Implicit Racial Bias in Public Defender Triage." *Yale Law Journal* 122: 13-24.

Rickard, Erika. 2017. "The Agile Court: Improving State Courts in the Service of Access to Justice and the Court User Experience." *Western New England Law Review* 39: 227-250.

Rickard, Erika, and Qudsiya Naqui. 2021. "Pandemic Spurs Technology Revolution in State Civil Courts." *Judicature* 105 (3): 2-3.

Ritchie, Jane, and Liz Spencer. 2002. "Qualitative Data Analysis for Applied Policy Research." In *Analyzing Qualitative Data*, edited by Alan Bryman and Bob Burgess, 173-194. Milton Park, UK: Routledge.

Rocco, Philip, Daniel Béland, and Alex Waddan. 2020. "Stuck in Neutral? Federalism, Policy Instruments, and Counter-Cyclical Responses to COVID-19 in the United States." *Policy & Society* 39 (3): 458-477.

Rosenberg, Maurice. 1971. "Judicial Discretion of the Trial Court, Viewed from Above." *Syracuse Law Review* 22 (3): 635–668.

Rossner, Meredith, and David Tait. 2023. "Presence and Participation in a Virtual Court." *Criminology & Criminal Justice* 23 (1): 135–157.

Ryan, John Paul, Allan Ashman, Bruce Dennis Sales, and Sandra Shane-DuBow. 1980. *American Trial Judges: Their Work Styles and Performance.* New York: Free Press.

Saam, Nicole J., and Wolfgang Kerber. 2013. "Policy Innovation, Decentralized Experimentation, and Laboratory Federalism." *Journal of Artificial Societies & Social Simulation* 16 (1): 1–15.

Saari, David J. 1976. "Modern Court Management: Trends in Court Organization Concepts—1976." *Justice System Journal* 2 (1): 19–33.

Sandefur, Rebecca L. 2016. "Paying down the Civil Justice Data Deficit: Leveraging Existing National Data Collection." *South Carolina Law Review* 68 (2): 295–310.

Sandefur, Rebecca L., and Emily Denne. 2022. "Access to Justice and Legal Services Regulatory Reform." *Annual Review of Law & Social Science* 18: 27–42.

Savchak, Elisha C., and Jennifer B. Bowie. 2016. "A Bottom-up Account of State Supreme Court Opinion Writing." *Justice System Journal* 37 (2): 94–114.

Schauffler, Richard Y. 2007. "Judicial Accountability in the US State Courts Measuring Court Performance." *Utrecht Law Review* 3: 112–128.

Schick, Allen. 2002. "Agencies in Search of Principles." *OECD Journal on Budgeting* 2 (1): 7–26.

Scott, Patrick G. 1997. "Assessing Determinants of Bureaucratic Discretion: An Experiment in Street-Level Decision Making." *Journal of Public Administration Research and Theory* 7 (1): 35–58.

Seawright, Jason, and John Gerring. 2008. "Case Selection Techniques in Case Study Research: A Menu of Qualitative and Quantitative Options." *Political Research Quarterly* 61 (2): 294–308.

Seidman-Diamond, Shari, Locke E. Bowman, Manyee Wong, and Matthew M. Patton. 2010. "Efficiency and Cost: The Impact of Videoconferenced Hearings on Bail Decisions." *Journal of Criminal Law and Criminology* 100 (3): 869–902.

Senden, Linda A. 2004. *Soft Law in European Community Law.* Oxford: Hart.

Shanahan, Colleen F., Anna E. Carpenter, and Alyx Mark. 2016. "Lawyers, Power, and Strategic Expertise." *Denver Law Review* 93: 469–521.

Shanahan, Colleen F., Alyx Mark, Jessica K. Steinberg, and Anna E. Carpenter. 2020. "Covid, Crisis, and Courts." *Texas Law Review Online* 99 (10): 10–19.

Shanahan, Colleen F., Jessica K. Steinberg, Alyx Mark, and Anna E. Carpenter. 2022a. "Lawyerless Law Development." *Stanford Law Review Online* 75 (1): 64–72.

————. 2022b. "The Institutional Mismatch of State Civil Courts." *Columbia Law Review* 122 (5): 1471–1537.

Shavell, Steven. 1995. "The Appeals Process as a Means of Error Correction." *Journal of Legal Studies* 24 (2): 379–426.

Shen, Wen. 2021. "Scope of CDC Authority under Section 361 of the Public Health Service Act (PHSA)." Report, Congressional Research Service, https://sgp.fas.org/crs/misc/R46758.pdf.

Smith, Christopher E., and Heidi Feldman. 2001. "Burdens of the Bench: State Supreme Courts' Non-Judicial Tasks." *Judicature* 84 (6): 304–309.

Snyder, Francis. 1994. "Soft Law and Institutional Practice in the European Community." In *The Construction of Europe: Essays in Honour of Emile Noël*, edited by Stephen Martin, 197–225. Dordrecht: Kluwer Academic.

Songer, Donald, Jeffery Segal, and Charles Cameron. 1994. "The Hierarchy of Justice: Testing a Principal-Agent Model of Supreme Court–Circuit Court Interactions." *American Journal of Political Science* 38 (3): 673–696.

Songer, Donald, and Reginald Sheehan. 1990. "Supreme Court Impact on Compliance and Outcomes: Miranda and *New York Times* in the United States Courts of Appeals." *Western Political Quarterly* 43 (2): 297–316.

Spaulding, Norman W. 2020. "The Ideal and the Actual in Procedural Due Process." *Hastings Constitutional Law Quarterly* 48: 261–296.

Spillane, Ed. 2021. "The End of Jury Trials: Covid-19 and the Courts: The Implications and Challenges of Holding Hearings Virtually and in Person during a Pandemic from a Judge's Perspective." *Ohio State Journal of Criminal Law* 18 (2): 537–554.

Spulak, Grace. 2024. *Remote Proceedings Toolkit, Version 2*. Williamsburg, VA: National Center for State Courts.

Stefan, O. 2020. "COVID-19 Soft Law: Voluminous, Effective, Legitimate? A Research Agenda." *European Papers—A Journal on Law and Integration* 5 (1): 663–670.

Steinberg, Jessica K. 2015. "Demand Side Reform in the Poor People's Court." *Connecticut Law Review* 47 (3): 741–805.

Stempel, Jeffrey W. 2001. "Politics and Sociology in Federal Civil Rulemaking: Errors of Scope." *Alabama Law Review* 52 (2): 529–637.

Sternlight, Jean R., and Jennifer K. Robbennolt. 2022. "In-Person or via Technology?: Drawing on Psychology to Choose and Design Dispute Resolution Processes." *DePaul Law Review:* 71 (2) 537–612.

Stott, E. Keith, Jr. 1982. "The Judicial Executive: Toward Greater Congruence in an Emerging Profession." *Justice System Journal* 7 (2): 152–179.

Subrin, Stephen N., and Thomas O. Main. 2016. "Breaking the Rules: Why State Courts Should Not Replicate Amendments to the Federal Rules of Civil Procedure." *Case Western Reserve Law Review* 67: 501–536.

Sudeall, Lauren, and Daniel Pasciuti. 2021. "Praxis and Paradox: Inside the Black Box of Eviction Court." *Vanderbilt Law Review* 74 (5): 1365–1434.

Tausanovitch, Chris, and Christopher Warshaw. 2013. "Measuring Constituent Policy Preferences in Congress, State Legislatures, and Cities." *Journal of Politics* 75 (2): 330–342.

Thatcher, Mark. 2002. "Delegation to Independent Regulatory Agencies: Pressures, Functions and Contextual Mediation." *West European Politics* 25 (1): 125–147.

———. 2005. "The Third Force? Independent Regulatory Agencies and Elected Politicians in Europe." *Governance* 18 (3): 347–373.

Tansey, Oisín. 2007. "Process Tracing and Elite Interviewing: A Case for Non-probability Sampling." *PS: Political Science & Politics* 40 (4): 765–772.

Thierer, Adam D. 2021. "Soft Law in US ICT Sectors: Four Case Studies." *Jurimetrics* 61 (1): 79–119.

Thumma, Samuel A., and Marcus W. Reinkensmeyer. 2022. "Post-pandemic Recommendations: COVID-19 Continuity of Court Operations during a Public Health Emergency Workgroup." *SMU Law Review Forum* 75 (1): 1–10.

Tobin, Robert. 1997. *An Overview of Court Administration in the United States.* Williamsburg, VA: National Center for State Courts.

Tobin, Robert, and John K. Hudzik. 1993. "The Status and Future of State Financing of Courts." In *The Handbook of Court Administration and Management*, edited by Steven W. Hays and Cole Blease Graham, 327–354. Philadelphia: Taylor and Francis.

Treskon, Mark, Solomon Greene, Olivia Fiol, and Anne Junod. 2021. "Eviction Prevention and Diversion Programs." Washington, DC: Urban Institute.

Tummers, Lars, Victor Bekkers, Evelien Vink, and Michael Musheno. 2015. "Coping during Public Service Delivery: A Conceptualization and Systematic Review of the Literature." *Journal of Public Administration Research and Theory* 25 (4): 1099–1126.

Turner, Jenia I. 2021. "Remote Criminal Justice." *Texas Tech Law Review* 53 (2): 197–271.

Van Slyke, David M. 2007. "Agents or Stewards: Using Theory to Understand the Government–Nonprofit Social Service Contracting Relationship." *Journal of Public Administration Research and Theory* 17 (2): 157–187.

Vedung, Evert. 1998. "Policy Instruments: Typologies and Theories." In *Carrots, Sticks, and Sermons: Policy Instruments and Their Evaluation*, edited by Marie-Louise Bemelmans-Videc and Ray C. Rist, 21–58. New York: Transaction.

Vining, Richard L., Jr., and Teena Wilhelm. 2023. *Administering Justice: Placing the Chief Justice in American State Politics.* Ann Arbor: University of Michigan Press.

Volden, Craig. 2006. "States as Policy Laboratories: Emulating Success in the Children's Health Insurance Program." *American Journal of Political Science* 50 (2): 294–312.

Wang, Qiang, Hong Hou, and Zhibin Li. 2022. "Participative Leadership: A Literature Review and Prospects for Future Research." *Frontiers in Psychology* 13: 1–12.

Weingast, Barry R. 2009. "Second Generation Fiscal Federalism: The Implications of Fiscal Incentives." *Journal of Urban Economics* 65 (3): 279–293.

Weinstein-Tull, Justin. 2020. "The Structures of Local Courts." *Virginia Law Review* 106 (5): 1031–1106.

Westerland, Chad, Jeffrey A. Segal, Lee Epstein, Charles M. Cameron, and Scott Comparato. 2010. "Strategic Defiance and Compliance in the US Courts of Appeals." *American Journal of Political Science* 54 (4): 891–905.

Xiao, Shiyang, and Xufeng Zhu. 2022. "Bureaucratic Control and Strategic Compliance: How Do Subnational Governments Implement Central Guidelines in China?" *Journal of Public Administration Research and Theory* 32 (2): 342–359.

Yeazell, Stephen C. 1994. "The Misunderstood Consequences of Modern Civil Process." *Wisconsin Law Review* 1994 (3): 631–678.

Zarnow, Zach, and Danielle Elyce Hirsch. 2021. "Inflection Point: Can Courts Use Technology to Spur Transformational Change, or Will They Return to the Traditional Way of Doing Business?" *Georgetown Law Technology Review* 5: 135–147.

Zhu, Xufeng, and Hu Zhao. 2018. "Experimentalist Governance with Interactive Central-Local Relations: Making New Pension Policies in China." *Policy Studies Journal* 49 (1): 13–36.

Index

task forces, function of, 70–71
technology in court systems
    control over tools and resources
        for, 63–66, 116–121
    in centralized states, 98–99
    measuring administrative power
        over use of, 51–57
    pre-pandemic, 117–18
    technology-related procedural
        changes for, 116, 130,
        144–147
    training for, 63–64
    See also electronic document
        management/electronic
        filing (e-filing); remote
        hearings
temporary policymaking, influence
    of administrative power
    on policy adoption in,
    109–113. See also emergency
    policymaking
Tennessee
    administrative centralization in,
        54
    remote-relevant administrative
        centralization in, 62, 114
    right to speedy trial in, 31
    state-level administrators'
        control in, 40, 41
    technology policies in, 66
    temporary rule changes in,
        66–67
Texas
    administrative power in, 53
    electronic filing management
        in, 121
    eviction diversion in, 138
    hearing modalities in, 128–129
    Remote Proceeding Task Force,
        128–129, 142
    remote-relevant administrative
        centralization in, 62, 114
    state-level administrators'
        control in, 40, 41, 42

training resources in, 64
training, 63–64, 65, 66, 76

Utah
    administrative centralization in,
        54
    information technology control
        in, 72
    local rulemaking in, 37
    lower court restrictions in, 72
    remote-relevant administrative
        centralization in, 62, 114
    right to speedy trial in, 31, 32
    state-level administrators'
        control in, 40
    uniform pandemic response in,
        72

vaccine mandates, 50
Vermont
    administrative centralization in,
        53, 54
    alternative dispute resolution
        (ADR) in, 145
    civil procedural rule change in,
        142
    document procedures in, 70
    electronic filing management
        in, 111, 115, 117, 118–119,
        120, 145
    hearing participation methods
        in, 142
    policy flexibility in, 115
    remote-relevant administrative
        centralization in, 62, 114
    Rule 43.1 in, 170n31
    rulemaking processes in, 131
    Rules for Electronic Filing in,
        145
    Rules of Civil Procedure in,
        146
    Special Advisory Committee on
        Remote Hearings, 143
    stakeholder groups in, 142

www.ingramcontent.com/pod-product-compliance
Ingram Content Group UK Ltd.
Pitfield, Milton Keynes, MK11 3LW, UK
UKHW042339210125
454002UK00013B/107/J

9 780700 638253